Break

Is not My Word like as a fire? saith the LORD; and like a hammer *that* breaketh the rock in pieces?
- Jeremiah 23:29.

THE CURSES

Moses Nsubuga Sekatawa

Break the curses

Moses Nsubuga Sekatawa

Copyright © 2012 by Moses Nsubuga Sekatawa

ISBN-10: **9970-883-04-6** (Uganda Publishers Ass'n)

Revised and reprinted in the United States of America.

Copyright © 2014 by Moses Nsubuga Sekatawa

ISBN-13: **978-1499505146**

ISBN-10: **1499505140**

Dedication

To Jessica, my darling wife, partner in ministry and faithful companion in life.

In Jesus' Name, I pray that you will continue to be all that God made you; a holy woman ablaze with the compassion and faith of God leading multitudes from the bondage of darkness to the glorious liberty of Jesus Christ our Lord and Saviour. I pray that you will continue to be God's intimate friend and that you will all the time obey Him and do His will for His glory, and your perfect joy! Let all your steps always be ordered by God and may you delight in His counsel all the days of your life. May no satanic scheme ever prevail against you in Jesus' Name!

Scriptural quotations are all derived from the Authorized (King James) Version of the Bible unless otherwise specified.

Sometimes they have been interpreted or simply alluded to, to suit individual application. Translations and paraphrases are all by me.

Needless to say, the nouns and pronouns by which satan and his cohorts are addressed do not bear any capital letters in this book unless it is a printing error.

Yours in Christ,

Moses Nsubuga Sekatawa.

Contents

Chapter 1.

A curse defined.

A curse may be defined in a number of ways. We will need to consider some few words from Hebrew and Greek so as to find out what the Bible means by a curse.

A. The word "curse" in Genesis 8:21 has been interpreted from "**qalal**"[1] which is the Hebrew equivalent of "abate", "bring into contempt", "accurse", "curse", "despise" and "lightly esteem".

---

[1] The New Strong's Exhaustive Concordance of the Bible, Hebrew Dictionary, page 126, word no. 7043.

1

21. And the LORD smelled a sweet savour; and the LORD said in his heart, I will not again curse the ground any more for man's sake; for the imagination of man's heart *is* evil from his youth; neither will I again smite any more every thing living, as I have done.

- Genesis 8:21.

B. The word "curse" in Genesis 12:3 has been translated from the Hebrew word "**arar**".[2] It means "to execrate", "to bitterly curse".

3. and I will bless them that bless thee, and curse him that curseth thee: and in thee shall all families of the earth be blessed.

- Genesis 12:3.

---

[2] The New Strong's Exhaustive Concordance of the Bible, Hebrew Dictionary, page 14, word no. 779.

C. The word "curse" in Genesis 27:12 is translated from the Hebrew word "**qelalah**".[3] It means "Vilification". To vilify is to speak ill about someone or something; to defame.

> 12. my father peradventure will feel me, and I shall seem to him as a deceiver; and I shall bring a curse upon me, and not a blessing.
>
> - Genesis 27:12.

D. The word "curse" in Numbers 5:21 has been translated from the Hebrew word "**alah**"[4] which means "an imprecation", "a curse", "cursing", "execration", "oath", "swearing", "to adjure in a bad sense".

> 21. then the priest shall charge the woman with an oath of cursing, and the priest shall say unto the woman, The LORD make thee a

---

[3] The New Strong's Exhaustive Concordance of the Bible, Hebrew Dictionary, page 126, word no. 7045.
[4] The New Strong's Exhaustive Concordance of the Bible, Hebrew Dictionary, page 8, word no 423.

curse and an oath among thy people, when the LORD doth make thy thigh to rot, and thy belly to swell;

- Numbers 5:21.

E. The word "curse" in Numbers 22:11 has been translated from the Hebrew word "**qabab**"[5] which means to "scoop out", "to malign", "to execrate", "to stab with words", "to curse".

11. Behold, *there is* a people come out of Egypt, which covereth the face of the earth: come now, curse me them; peradventure I shall be able to overcome them, and drive them out.

- Numbers 22:11.

F. In Joshua 6:18 the word "curse" has

---

[5] The New Strong's Exhaustive Concordance of the Bible, Hebrew Dictionary, page 123, word no. 6895.

4

been translated from "**cherem**".[6] It refers to "a secluded thing", "something banned", "something appointed to utter destruction".

> 18. And ye, in any wise keep *yourselves* from the accursed thing, lest ye make *yourselves* accursed, when ye take of the accursed thing, and make the camp of Israel a curse, and trouble it.
>
> - Joshua 6:18.

G. The word "curse" in Job 2:9 is translated from the Hebrew word "**barak**"[7], which means to kneel, by implication to bless God (*as an act of adoration*) and (*vice versa*) man (*as a benefit*). Also by euphemism to curse (*God or the king, as treason*) to blaspheme, bless, congratulate, curse, kneel down, praise, salute, thank.

---

[6] The New Strong's Exhaustive Concordance of the Bible, Hebrew Dictionary, page 48, word no. 2764.
[7] The New Strong's Exhaustive Concordance of the Bible, Hebrew Dictionary, page 23, word no 1288.

> 9. Then said his wife unto him, Dost thou still retain thine integrity? curse God, and die.
>
> - Job 2:9.

H. In Numbers 23:8 the word "curse" is from the Hebrew term "**naqab**"[8] which means to puncture, literally (*to perforate with more or less violence*) or figuratively (*to specify, designate, libel*):- appoint, blaspheme, bore, curse, express with holes, name, pierce, strike through.

> **8.** How shall I curse, whom God hath not cursed? or how shall I defy, *whom* the LORD hath not defied?
>
> - Numbers 23:8.

I. In Lamentations 3:65 the word "curse" is from the Hebrew word "**ta'alah**"[9] which means "an imprecation", "a curse".

---

[8] The New Strong's Exhaustive Concordance of the Bible, Hebrew Dictionary, page 96, word no. 5344.
[9] The New Strong's Exhaustive Concordance of the Bible, Hebrew Dictionary, page 150, word no.8381

65.   Give them sorrow of heart,
thy curse unto them.

- Lamentations 3:65.

J.   The word "curse" in Proverbs 3:33 is translated from the Hebrew word "**merah**"[10] which means "an imprecation", "a curse".

33.   The curse of the LORD *is* in
the house of the wicked: but he
blesseth the habitation of the just.

- Proverbs 3:33.

K.   In Matthew 5:44 the word "curse" is from the Greek word "**kataraomai**"[11] which means "to execrate", "to doom". To execrate means to express or feel abhorrence for someone or something, to utter curses.

---

[10] The New Strong's Exhaustive Concordance of the Bible, Hebrew Dictionary, page 71, word no.3994.
[11] The New Strong's Exhaustive Concordance of the Bible, Greek Dictionary, page 47, word no.2672.

44.   But I say unto you, Love your enemies, bless them that curse you, do good to them that hate you, and pray for them which despitefully use you, and persecute you;

- Matthew 5:44.

L.   In Mark 14:71 the word "curse" is translated from **"anathematizo"**,[12] a Greek word which means, "to declare" or vow under penalty of execration:- (bind under a) curse, bind with an oath. It is derived from the Greek word "anathema"[13] which means an excommunicated person or thing, accursed. Something banned religiously.

71.   But he began to curse and to swear, *saying*, I know not this man of whom ye speak.

- Mark 14:71.

---

[12] The New Strong's Exhaustive Concordance of the Bible, Greek Dictionary, page 6, word no.332.
[13] The New Strong's Exhaustive Concordance of the Bible, Greek Dictionary, page 6, word no.331.

M. In Matthew 26:74 the word "curse" is translated from **"kathanathematizo"**,[14] a Greek word that means to imprecate. To imprecate is to invoke evil upon someone or something.

> 74. Then began he to curse and to swear, *saying*, I know not the man. And immediately the cock crew.
>
> - Matthew 26:74.

N. In Galatians 3:13 the word "curse" is translated from the Greek word, **"katara"**.[15] It means an imprecation and an execration.

> 13. Christ hath redeemed us from the curse of the law, being made a curse for us: for it is written, Cursed *is* every one that hangeth on a tree:
>
> - Galatians 3:13.

---

[14] The New Strong's Exhaustive Concordance of the Bible, Greek Dictionary, page 47, word no.2653.
[15] The New Strong's Exhaustive Concordance of the Bible, Greek Dictionary, page 47, word no.2671.

O. The word "curse" in Revelation 22:3 is translated from the Greek word, **"katanathema"**[16] It means "an imprecation" "a curse".

> 3. And there shall be no more curse: but the throne of God and of the Lamb shall be in it; and his servants shall serve him:
>
> - Revelation 22:3.

Having considered some few words in Hebrew and Greek, I would like to conclude by defining a "curse" in five ways:

i. God's just reward in the life of a person and their descendants because of iniquity.

ii. Negative words spoken by an authority to invoke evil over a person, a group of people, a place or a thing to

---

[16] The New Strong's Exhaustive Concordance of the Bible, Greek Dictionary, page 47, word no.2652.

alter its course and deter or hinder its would be positive progress.

iii. Blasphemous, "stabbing" words spoken by an inferior to a superior. Job's wife asked him to curse God.[17] The Bible warns us against cursing our parents.[18]

iv. An accusing voice in the courts of heavens crying out for justice and vengeance against an individual or a bloodline because of unrepented sins and unbroken evil covenants.

v. A strong spiritual force, which hinders one's positive progress in life robbing them of their life, joy, strength, resources and every virtuous treasure, piercing and puncturing, or perforating their hearts with many sorrows.

---

[17] Job 2:9.
[18] Exodus 21:17; Leviticus 20:9; Proverbs 20:20; Matthew 15:4; Mark 7:10.

Chapter 2.

Sin, transgression, iniquity, and abomination

The major reason for a curse is always one, UNRIGHTEOUSNESS. This brings me to some things I should explain in detail. What is sin? What is a transgression? What is iniquity? What is an abomination?

1. What is sin?

Every act of unbelief is sin.

23.   And he that doubteth is damned if he eat, because *he eateth* not of faith: for whatsoever *is* not faith is sin.

- Romans 14:23.

Sin includes all evil ideas, acts and every form unrighteousness and rebellion against God.

17.   All unrighteousness is sin: and there is a sin not unto death.

- 1 John 5:17.

2.   What is a transgression?

3.   Then the kings servants, which *were* in the king's gate, said unto Mordecai, Why transgressest thou the king's commandment?

- Esther 3:3.

11. Yea, all Israel have transgressed thy law, even by departing, that they might not obey thy voice; therefore the curse is poured upon us, and the oath that *is* written in the law of Moses the servant of God, because we have sinned against Him.

- Daniel 9:11.

4. Whosoever committeth sin transgresseth also the law: for sin is the transgression of the law.

- 1 John 3: 4.

When we break the law, commandments or ordinances of God then we have transgressed. Every transgression is a sin.

3. What is iniquity?

18. If I regard iniquity in my

heart, the Lord will not hear *me:*

- Psalm 66:18.

15. Thou wast perfect in thy ways from the day that thou wast created, till iniquity was found in thee.

- Ezekiel 28:15.

Iniquity refers to the moral wickedness of the heart; perversity. Sometimes we do not discern iniquity until a person is exposed to temptation. lucifer's heart was lifted up because of his beauty.[1] How was his iniquity discerned? Isaiah tells the story:

13. For thou hast said in thine heart, I will ascend into heaven, I will exalt my throne above the stars

---

[1] Ezekiel 28:17.

of God: I will sit also upon the mount of the congregation, in the sides of the north:

14. I will ascend above the heights of the clouds; I will be like the Most High.

15. Yet thou shalt be brought down to hell, to the sides of the pit.

- Isaiah 14:13–15.

Iniquity was in lucifer's heart. lucifer met the judgment of God. Our hearts speak loudly to God. He hears the voices of our hearts God looks at the heart.[2] The Psalmist cried, "Let the words of my mouth, and the meditation of my heart be acceptable in thy sight, O LORD, my Strength, and my Redeemer".[3]

---

[2] 1 Samuel 16:17.
[3] Psalm 19:14.

Iniquity is that deposit of filth in a heart, out of which when temptations come along, little ugly stenches arise. It is those stenches, which we call sin. Iniquity can be inherited. It is very easy for wicked parents to raise up a generation of wicked children.

Not every sin is at level of iniquity. When we succumb to temptation, enticed by our desires, then we have sinned.[4] When we sin then we transgress (break) the laws.[5] When that becomes a way of life; our hearts desire, then it has got to the stage of iniquity.[6] Someone does not feel guilty whether they tell a lie or fornicate. The counsel of God no longer matters to them; their conscience is as though seared with a hot iron.[7] He or she may appear honourable outwardly but "as he thinketh in his heart, so is he".[8]

---

[4] James 1:13-16.
[5] 1 John 3:4.
[6] Jeremiah 17:9.
[7] 1 Timothy 4:1-2.
[8] Proverbs 23:7.

When we come to the stage of iniquity and our cup is full to the brim, then the judgment of God is inevitable.[9] God judges iniquity. Those who choose to walk in it suffer the consequences of that judgment.[10]

4.   What is an abomination?

Once again we will have to study a few words from the Hebrew and one word in Greek to get a clearer picture of what the Bible calls an abomination.

A.   The Hebrew word for abomination in Leviticus 18:22 is "**towebah**"[11] or "**toebah**". It means something morally disgusting, an abhorrence. For example, homosexuality is an abomination; so is lesbianism and bestiality. God abhors and detests them. He regards

---

[9] 1 Corinthians 11:31-32.
[10] Exodus 20:5.
[11] The New Strong's Exhaustive Concordance of the Bible, Hebrew Dictionary, Page 151, word no. 8441.

them filthy practices. He destroyed Sodom and Gomorrah just because of homosexuality. Perhaps that's why He did not make Adam and Steve, He made Adam and Eve!

> 22. Thou shalt not lie with mankind, as with womankind: it *is* an abomination.
>
> - Leviticus 18:22.

B. The Hebrew word for abomination in Leviticus 7:18 is "**pigguwl**".[12] It means to stink, something fetid, ceremonially unclean. It means something abominable.

> 18. And if *any* of the flesh of the sacrifice of his peace offerings be eaten at all on the third day, it shall not be accepted, neither shall it be

---

[12] The New Strong's Exhaustive Concordance of the Bible, Hebrew Dictionary, Page 112, word no. 6292.

imputed unto him that offereth it: it shall be an abomination, and the soul that eateth of it shall bear his iniquity:

- Leviticus 7:18.

C.   There are two Hebrew words, used for abomination in Leviticus 11:10-11. The first word, "an abomination" is from Hebrew word **"sheqets"**.[13]   It means filth, an idolatrous object, something abominable, an abomination. The second word, "in abomination" is **"shaqats"**.[14] It means to be filthy, to loathe, to pollute. To abhor or make abominable, have in abomination, utterly detest.

> 10.   And all that have not fins and scales in the seas, and in the rivers, of all that move in the waters, and of any living thing

---

[13] The New Strong's Exhaustive Concordance of the Bible, Hebrew Dictionary, Page 148, word no. 8263.
[14] The New Strong's Exhaustive Concordance of the Bible, Hebrew Dictionary, Page 148, word no. 8262.

which is in the waters, they shall be an abomination into you:

11. They shall be even an abomination unto you; ye shall not eat of their flesh, but ye shall have their carcases in abomination.

- Leviticus 11:10-11.

D. The Hebrew word used for abomination in 1 Samuel 13:3-4 is "**ba'ash**".[15] It means to smell bad, to make or be loathsome, odious, abhorred. It means to cause a stink. It means to be morally offensive. It appears once in the Bible.

3. And Janathan smote the garrison of the Philistines that was in Geba, and the Philistines heard of it. And Saul blew the trumpet throughout all the land, saying, Let the Hebrews hear.

---

[15] The New Strong's Exhaustive Concordance of the Bible, Hebrew Dictionary, Page 16, word no. 887.

4.   And all Israel heard say that Saul had smitten a garrison of the Philistines, and that Israel also was had in abomination with the Philistines. And the people were called together after Saul to Gilgal.

E.   The Hebrew word for abomination in 1 Kings 11:7-8 is "**shiqquwts**" or "**shiqquts**".[16] It means something disgusting, filthy, and especially idolatrous. For example an idol is an abominable filth and a detestable thing before God.

7.   Then did Solomon build an high place for Chemosh, the abomination of Moab, in the hill that is before Jerusalem, and for Molech, the abomination of the children of Ammon.

---

[16] The New Strong's Exhaustive Concordance of the Bible, Hebrew Dictionary, Page 147, word no. 8251.

23

8.   And likewise did he for all his strange wives, which burnt incense and sacrificed unto their gods.

- 1 Kings 11:7-8.

F.   The Greek word translated to mean abomination is **"bdelugma"**.[17]   It means a detestation,   an   abomination,   something disgusting in the sight of God such as idolatry.

From the scriptures we discover that some sins such as idolatry and sexual perversions are disgusting in the sight of God. They grieve the heart of God and make the culprit a filthy, stinking spectacle before Him.

God rewards righteousness and obedience with the anointing[18] and with blessings.[19]   He

---

[17] The New Strong's Exhaustive Concordance of the Bible, Greek Dictionary, Page 17, word no. 946.
[18] Psalms 45:7; Hebrews 1:9.
[19] Deuteronomy 28:1-14, Isaiah 1:19.

recompenses unrighteousness and disobedience to Him with curses.[20]

14. And the Pharisees also, who were covetous, heard all these things: and they derided him.

15. And he said unto them, Ye are they, which justify yourselves before men; but God knoweth your hearts: for that which is highly esteemed among men is abomination in the sight of God.

- Luke 16:14–15.

27. And there shall in no wise enter into it any thing that defileth, neither whatsoever worketh an abomination, or *maketh* a lie: but they which are written in the

---

[20] Deuteronomy 28:15–68, Isaiah 1:20.

Lamb's book of life.

- Revelation 21:27.

Chapter 3.

Why curses?

Some people have lived under a curse because of their own wickedness or because of the wickedness of their ancestors and spouses.[1] What we do in life has the potential not only to affect us, but also to affect our spouses and children.

> 4. Thou shalt not make unto thee any graven image, or any *likeness of any thing* that *is* in

---

[1] Exodus 20:5; Jeremiah 32:18; Proverb 26:2; Lamentations 5:7

heaven above, or that *is* in the earth beneath, or that *is* in the water under the earth.

5.   Thou shalt not bow down thyself to them, nor serve them: for I the LORD thy God *Am* a Jealous God, visiting the iniquity of the fathers upon the children unto the third and fourth *generation* of them that hate Me;

- Exodus 20:4–5.

6.   And the LORD passed by before him, and proclaimed, The LORD, The LORD God, merciful and gracious,   longsuffering,   and abundant in goodness and truth,

7.   Keeping   mercy   for thousands, forgiving iniquity and transgression and sin, and that will by no means clear the guilty;

visiting the iniquity of the fathers upon the children, and upon the children's children, unto the third and to the fourth generation.

- Exodus 34:7.

17.   Ah Lord God! behold, thou hast made the heaven and the earth by thy great power and stretched out arm, and there is nothing too hard for thee:

18.   Thou   shewest lovingkindness unto thousands: and recompensest the iniquity of the fathers into the bosom of their children after them: the Great, the Mighty God, the LORD of hosts, is His Name,   .

19.   Great in counsel, and mighty in work: for Thine eyes are open upon all the ways of the sons of

men: to give every one according to his ways, and according to the fruit of his doings:

- Jeremiah 32:16-19.

7.   Our fathers have sinned, and are not; and we have borne their iniquities.

- Lamentation 5:7.

6.   My people are destroyed for lack of knowledge: because thou hast rejected knowledge, I will also reject thee, that thou shalt be no priest to Me: seeing thou hast forgotten the law of thy God, I will also forget thy children.

- Hosea 4:6.

According to these verses, God does not wink at unrighteousness. Sin does not only affect the culprit who commits it. Its repercussions reverberate to the future generations of the people in the culprit's bloodline.

I have met a number of people who go through adverse circumstances or an evil cycle of defeat. The reason for the bondage of many of them was what their ancestors did. The moment the sins of their ancestors were confessed and the evil covenants which had been established by those ancestors were broken, the demons lost their legal ground. Deliverance became very easy.

God's punishment for iniquity would have stopped on the third and fourth generation.[2] The trouble is that the descendants often end up guilty of the same sins as their ancestors. Therefore, the curse continues down the bloodline until someone stops it by repentance[3] and by exercising our God given authority because of Calvary.[4]

Cain murdered his brother.[5] Later on in life Cain's descendant slew him.[6] Cain's evil

---

[2] Exodus 20:5; Exodus 34:7; Jeremiah 32:18; Lamentations 5:7; Hosea 4:6.
[3] Nehemiah 9:1-3.
[4] Luke 10:19; John 14:14.
[5] Genesis 4:8.
[6] Genesis 4:23.

action opened the door for blood thirsty demons to enter into his life and bloodline.

How does a curse open the door for demons?

A curse brings about sorrow in the heart of the accursed.[7] It robs a person of their God given joy. It causes frustration and adversity. A curse hinders a person's positive progress in anything they try to do. It defies all physical, emotional, and intellectual defences. One cannot have complete joy while labouring under a curse.

Complete joy is always the result of answered prayers.[8] The joy of the Lord is our strength.[9] God is a joyful God.[10] In His presence is fullness of joy.[11] We run the risk of hosting sorrow when we lose the joy of the Lord.

---

[7] Genesis 4:13-14.
[8] John 16:24.
[9] Nehemiah 8:10.
[10] Zephaniah 3:17.
[11] Psalm 16:11.

Sorrow is the opposite of joy. Just as joy strengthens us and ushers the presence of God into our lives.[12] Sorrow drives all strength away. When all defences are broken down, the person becomes helpless as far as demonic attacks are concerned.

Every stressful or traumatic experience in the life of an individual can serve as a door for demons to enter into that person's life.

When demons enter into a person's life, they perpetuate their evil programmes against that person and his defenceless loved ones.

Therefore, a curse brings about sorrow. Sorrow weakens a person and therefore opens the door of his life to demonic spirits to enter therein. They may be spirits of fear. With fear comes torment.[13] The end result of that person is destruction.

---

[12] Psalm 22:3; Ephesians 5:18-20.
[13] 1 John 4:18.

Some evil spirits will not come out of certain people until curses are broken.

Can a curse affect you without a cause?

> 2.   As the bird by wondering, as the swallow by flying, so the curse causeless shall not come.
>
> - Proverbs 26:2.

According to Proverbs 26:2, a person cannot be affected by a curse unless there is a cause for it. Sometimes the conduct of that person may be ungodly and so the cause of problems. It may be that person's family. Someone can inherit a demon or disease from his family.

When one deviates from God's standard of how life should be lived, then painful to say, that person has strayed away from the territory of our security and blessings to the territory of insecurity and curses. According to the Bible God has given us the right to choose life or death, blessings or curses and our choices affect us and our off springs.[14]

For every truth of God presented to us, satan tries to come up with an attractive counterfeit. For example, we know that Jesus Christ, the Son of the Living God is the only way to eternal life[15] but we are also warned in Proverbs 14:12 and 16:12 about a counterfeit:

> 12.   There   is   a   way   which seemeth right unto a man, but the end thereof are the ways of death.
>
>   - Proverb 14:12.

> 25.   There is a way that seemeth right   unto   a   man,   but   the   end thereof are the ways of death.
>
>   - Proverbs 16:25.

---

[14] Deuteronomy 30:19.
[15] John 14:6; Acts 4:12.

The Bible warns us about perverted ways. It is these perverted ways, which lead people away from the mercy and grace of God to death and destruction.

> 18. Whoso walketh uprightly shall be saved: but he that is perverse in his ways shall fall at once.
>
> - Proverb 28:18.

Perverseness and iniquity are sure to be found at the root of curses.

We hear some of God's children quote Numbers 23:23 and affirm; "Surely there is no enchantment against Jacob, neither is there any divination against Israel". It is interesting to note that the verse begins with "SURELY". This means its strength is anchored in the preceding verses. It is important for us to study this verse within its rightful context.

19.   God is not a man, that he should lie; neither the son of man, that he should repent: hath he said, and shall he not do it? or hath he spoken, and shall he not make it good?

20.   Behold, I have received commandment to bless: and he hath blessed; and I cannot reverse it.

21.   hath not beheld iniquity in Jacob, neither hath he seen perverseness in Israel: the Lord his God is with him, and the shout of a king is among them.

22.   God brought them out of Egypt; he hath as it were the strength of an unicorn.

23.   Surely   there   is   no enchantment against Jacob, neither is there any divination against Israel: according to this time it shall be said of Jacob and of Israel, What hath God wrought!

- Numbers 23:19-23.

The reason for no divination and no enchantment is because of what is mentioned in the twenty first verse; **hath not beheld iniquity** and **hath not seen perverseness**.

SOME OF THE PERVERTED WAYS

1.   Perverted sexuality

This includes all acts of sexual sins, for example adultery, fornication, incest, bestiality, homosexuality, lesbianism, oral sex, anal sex, pornography, sexual lust of the eyes and of the flesh, sexual fantasies, sexual orgies, rape, paedophilia, molestation, masturbation, and any other means of seeking to obtain sexual pleasure or satisfaction contrary to the prescribed Bible bounds of a holy marriage.[16]

Sexual sins bring about the judgment of God. They open the door for curses to operate in the lives and bloodline of the culprits. God has called us to be holy in all that we think, speak, and do.[17] That is the key to joy and victory in life.[18]

2. Perverted family order

God intended the man to be the head of the family just like Christ is the head of the Church.[19] The man is obliged to love his wife and to protect, and defend his family while giving them a sense of direction.[20] He should be the vision bearer, so to speak.

The family where our Lord Jesus was born was such an ideal example. Jesus was the

---

[16] Hebrews 13:4.
[17] Ephesians 1:4; 1 Peter 1:15-17; Philippians 2:12-15, 4:8.
[18] Ephesians 5:22:25.
[19] Ephesians 5:22-24.
[20] Ephesians 5:25-33; 6:4.

Word made flesh.[21] He was God with us.[22] He was God manifest in the flesh.[23] Mary too was such a godly woman. She knew what it meant to converse with an angel sent from God. Her speech after the angelic visit indicated that she had deep knowledge of the Word of God.[24] She was highly favoured. The Lord was with her. She was blessed among women.[25] She had found favour with God.[26] Then there was Joseph, the carpenter. It always took Joseph some sleep before he would receive a message from God.[27]

Yet Joseph's household was not a child-centred institute. Jesus was subject to Joseph and Mary.[28] Mary did not dominate the household either. Even in her talk, she mentioned Joseph first.[29] She was submissive to Joseph. Joseph loved his wife

---

[21] John 1:1-14.
[22] Matthew 1:23.
[23] 1 Timothy 3:16.
[24] Luke 1:26-38, 46-55.
[25] Luke 1:28-30.
[26] Luke 1:30.
[27] Matthew 1:18-20; 2:13-14 & 2:19-21.
[28] Luke 2:51-52.
[29] Luke 2:48.

and 'son'. He forsook his business and went to exile for the sake of his family's security.[30] God used to give the major plans of this family, not to Jesus, not Mary but to Joseph the head of the family. Joseph was subject to the counsel of the Lord.

When the God-ordained order of the family is distorted all you end up with are men who fail to love, protect and guide their families. They decline from the assumption of leadership roles just as Ahab did. You end up with nagging, dominating females just like Jezebel[31] or Herodias[32] were. When the home becomes child-centred, the parents and guests become hostages to the carnal desires and priorities of those ungodly children.

We are instructed to train our children up in the way they should go.[33] We should bring our children up in the fear of God.[34] We are told not to spare the rod, but to chasten our

---

[30] Matthew 2:13-14.
[31] 1 Kings 19:1-2; 1 Kings 21: 1-15.
[32] Matthew 14:9-11.
[33] Proverb 22:6.
[34] Ephesians 6:4.

children.[35] Of course, we should not be blind to the fact that in some homes there is a very thin line between the rod of correction and child abuse. We need to differentiate the rod of correction from brutality.

A perverted family order hinders God's blessing and opens the door for curses to operate in a household,[36] and finally in the bloodline.

3.   Financial sins

God is so much interested in the way we obtain and spend our money. The Word of God stands firmly against unjust gain, taking advantage of others selfishly, cheating, extortion, gambling, and covetousness. It is sinful to be involved in crooked means of obtaining money and property, theft, mishandling of church finances, robbing God of the whole tithe and of offerings,[37] misuse of money, squandering, and any other form of financial unrighteousness.

---

[35] Proverb 13:24; 22:15; 13:14; 29:15.
[36] Proverb 3:33.
[37] Malachi 3:8-10.

God is so much interested in what we give, how we give, and why we give.[38] God is interested in the percentages we give.[39]

A history of any manifestations of financial wickedness in the bloodline has the potential to open the door for curses of poverty.

Worship of money and wealth,[40] materialism,[41] not honouring financial pledges and telling lies to God and the brethren about money is sinful.[42]

4. False religious systems

> 26. If any man among you seem to be religious, and bridleth not his tongue, but deceiveth his own heart, this man's religion is vain.

---

[38] Mark 12:41; 4:4; Luke 21:1-4.
[39] Luke 6:38.
[40] Matthew 6:19-34.
[41] 1 Timothy 6:5–10.
[42] Acts 5:1-11; Ecclesiastes 5:4-6.

27. Pure religion and undefiled before God and the Father is this, To visit the fatherless and widows in their affliction, and to keep himself unspotted from the world.

- James 1:26-27

In the two verses we have just quoted the Bible talks about some vain religions. There is also *"pure religion and undefiled before God"*. It demands that we bridle our tongues, that we do not allow our hearts to be deceived, that we minister to the orphans and widows with the God-kind of love, and that we keep ourselves unspotted from the world.

We know from the scriptures that the only way to keep ourselves pure and unspotted from the world is to run to Jesus and allow His blood to wash all our sins away.[43] Then we let His blood cleanse us every moment of our

---

[43] Romans 3:23-26; Hebrews 9:13-14.

lives.[44]   Pure religion and undefiled before God cannot therefore be a system of worship concocted by humanity.   It is SALVATION, when our lives become God's dwelling place,[45] and His presence becomes our dwelling place.[46]   Our abilities and talents cannot qualify us. It has to be by the grace of God.[47]

Any system of worship, whose foundation is not Jesus Christ the Son of the living God, is false.[48]

It is an evil thing to worship idols,[49] living or dead people,[50] angels,[51] or any creature whether in heaven, on earth, in the sea, in hell or anywhere else.[52]   We should stay away from any teaching, which offers a hope of salvation outside the provisions of Calvary.[53]

---

[44] 1 John 1:6-9.
[45] 1 Corinthians 3:16-17; 6:19-20; Philippians 2:12-13; Psalm 91:1.
[46] 2 Corinthians 6:16.
[47] Ephesians 2:5-6; Ephesians 2:8.
[48] 1 Corinthians 3:11.
[49] Leviticus 19:4; 26:1; 1 Kings 21:26.
[50] Leviticus 19:28; Deuteronomy 18:11; Acts 12:21-23; 14:11-18.
[51] Colossians 2:18; Revelation 19:10.
[52] Exodus 20:3-5.
[53] Colossians 2:8.

No human being ever solved the sin problem and no one will ever solve it. We have all sinned and come short of the glory of God.[54] We all need help. Hail Mary cannot save us[55] because she too needed a saviour.[56] Saint Peter cannot help us because he also acknowledged his helplessness before the Lord.[57] There is only one solution to the sin problem. That solution is Jesus Christ.[58] He is the Lamb of God![59]

False religious systems are an abomination before God. They open the life of a person and his descendants to multiple curses.

5. Perverted spirituality

Whenever a person seeks spiritual solutions outside the counsel of God, that person opens the door of his or her life to ungodly spirits to

---

[54] Romans 3:23.
[55] Acts 4:12.
[56] Luke 1:47.
[57] Luke 5:1-9.
[58] John 3:16; Matthew 1:21.
[59] John 1:29, 36.

influence their lives. When God speaks to us, His spoken Word is always in agreement with the scriptures. The Spirit of God cannot give us any counsel that is contrary to the scriptures He inspired[60] because God is not the author of confusion.[61] The scriptures are God's inspired Word.[62] They testify of the Living Word, Jesus Christ on the Father's right hand.[63] The word of God stands firmly against magical arts,[64] enchantments,[65] wicthcraft,[66] sorcery,[67] soothsaying,[68] divination,[69] wizardly,[70] necromancy,[71] magic,[72] charms,[73] prognostication,[74] observing times,[75] astrology and star gazing.[76] Any submission to the counsel of demons contradicts the Word of God because as many

---

[60] 1 Peter 1:21.
[61] 1 Corinthians 14:33.
[62] 2 Timothy 3:16.
[63] John 5:39.
[64] Exodus 7:11-13.
[65] Leviticus 19:26; 2 Chronicles 33:6; Jeremiah 27:9.
[66] Exodus 22:15; Nahum 3:14; Micah 5:122; Kings 9:22.
[67] Isaiah 47:9; Malachi 3:15; Acts 13:6-12.
[68] Isaiah 2:16; Daniel 2:27; Micah 5:12.
[69] Numbers 22:7; Ezekiel 12:24.
[70] Leviticus 19:31, 20:6; 2 Kings 21:1-6.
[71] Deuteronomy 18:9-12:7-20; 1 Samuel 28; Isaiah 8:19.
[72] Genesis 41:8, 24; Acts 19:18-20.
[73] Deuteronomy 18:9-12; Isaiah 19:3.
[74] Isaiah 47:12-15.
[75] Leviticus 19:26; 2 Kings 21:6; 2 Chronicles 33:6.
[76] Isaiah 47:13; Jeremiah 10:2; Daniel: 2:2, 10-11, 4:7, 5:7-15.

as are led by the Spirit of God; they are the sons of God.[77]   Any involvement by an individual or a group of people in voodoo, the occult and spiritism or any of the above-mentioned sins submits a person or a group of people to the lordship of the powers of darkness.[78]   A history of these sins the bloodline can open the door for multiple curses. It is actually impossible to break the first three commandments and get off scot-free (Exodus 20:7).

6.   Ungodly conduct

16.   These   six *things* doth   the LORD   hate: yea,   seven *are* an abomination unto Him:

17.   A proud look, a lying tongue, and   hands   that   shed   innocent blood,

---

[77] 1 Chronicles10:13; Romans 8:14.
[78] Romans 6:16.

18. An heart that deviseth wicked imaginations, feet that be swift in running to mischief,

19. A false witness *that* speaketh lies, and he that soweth discord among brethren.

- Proverbs 6:16-19.

19. Now the works of the flesh are manifest, which are *these*; Adultery, fornication, uncleanness, lasciviousness,

20. Idolatry, witchcraft, hatred, variance, emulations, wrath, strife, seditions, heresies,

21. Envyings, murders, drunkenness, revellings, and such like: of the which I tell you before, as I have also told *you* in time past, that they which do such things

shall not inherit the kingdom of
God.

22.　　But the fruit of the Spirit is
love, joy, peace, longsuffering,
gentleness, goodness, faith,

　　　　　　　- Galatians 5:19-22.

1.　　This know also, that in the
last days perilous times shall
come.

2.　　For men shall be lovers of
their own selves, covetous,
boasters, proud, blasphemers,
disobedient to parents, unthankful,
unholy,

3.　　Without natural affection,
trucebreakers, false accusers,
incontinent, fierce, despisers of
those that are good,

4. Traitors, heady, highminded, lovers of pleasures more than lovers of God;

- 2 Timothy 3:1–4.

Ungodly conduct includes every perverse way. Any sin described by the three scriptural quotations listed[79] and so much more. A history of such ungodly conduct displeases God and opens the life of an individual, a family, or a bloodline to curses.[80]

7. Perverse speech

21. Death and life *are* in the power of the tongue: and they that love it shall eat the fruit thereof.

- Proverbs 18: 21.

---

[79] Proverbs 6:16-19; Galatians 5:19-21; 2 Timothy 3:1–4.
[80] Proverbs 3:33.

37.   For by thy words thou shalt be justified, and by thy words thou shalt be condemned.

- Matthew 12:37.

Words are so important. All things were created by speech.[81] All things are upheld by speech.[82] We are saved by words.[83]

We are justified by words.[84] By words some are condemned.[85] Everyone is where they are in life because of what they speak, hear, and believe.[86] It is all about words. By our words, we can minister grace to the hearers and to ourselves.[87] Prayer is, but words.[88] Words may be invisible, but affect our yesterday, today and eternity.

---

[81] John 1:3.
[82] Hebrews 1:3.
[83] Romans 10:9–10.
[84] Matthew 12:37; Romans 10:9-10.
[85] Matthew 12:37.
[86] Mark 11:22-24.
[87] Ephesians 4:29.
[88] Matthew 6:7-13.

Perverse speech includes every form of corrupt ungodly set of words, profanity, jesting, swearing, cursing, enchantment, bewitchments, blasphemy, vexes, hexes, spells, lying, libel, slander, vows, oath, pledges and commitments made to demons, rumour mongering, obscene language et cetera.

By use of our tongues, we can either please or displease God.[89] Some parents curse their children by speaking negative words into their lives, either carelessly or when angered. Some people curse their businesses and God-given dreams and blessings by speaking words contrary to the counsel of God.[90]

Job's words invited trouble into his life and family.[91] Zacharias would have aborted God's plan for his life by speaking words of unbelief. There was need for him to be dumb until the

---

[89] James 3:1-18.
[90] Numbers 13:1-3.
[91] Job 3:26.

birth of his son; John the Baptist.[92]

Ungodly speech denies an individual, a family, or a bloodline the privilege of enjoying God's blessings. It can usher a whole bloodline into bondage and curses. There are families today that labour under the burden of curses just because of words said by their ancestors.

Goliath was a champion of the armies of the Philistines. His people allowed him to speak on their behalf. He came in their name and in the names of all the evil forces which stood against Israel in that war. He invoked all the powers of darkness which favoured the Philistine cause against Israel. He pledged that he and all his people would be servants to Israel in case he was defeated. Of course, Mr. Goliath and his gods were defeated. The covenant of their defeat was sealed in his own blood. Those same words still work against everyone from his camp who wars against Israel.[93]

---

[92] Luke 1:5–20.
[93] 1 Samuel 17:1-51.

We are told not to be rash with our mouths.[94] We should *"be swift to hear, slow to speak, slow to wrath".*[95]

The Psalmist cried:

> 14.   Let the words of my mouth, and the meditation of my heart, be acceptable in thy sight, O LORD, my Strength, and my Redeemer.
>
> - Psalm 19:14.

8.   Ungodly   associations, environments and influences

> 1.   Blessed *is* the   man   that walketh not in the counsel of the ungodly, nor standeth in the way of

---

[94] Ecclesiastes 5:2.
[95] James 1:19.

sinners, nor sitteth in the seat of the scornful.

2.   But his delight *is* in the law of the LORD; and in his law doth he meditate day and night.

- Psalm 1:1–2.

In this context, the word "ungodly" is translated from the Hebrew word "**rasha**".[96] It refers to someone morally wrong, an actively bad person, condemned, guilty, ungodly, a wicked person that is associated with doing wrong.   The word "sinners" is in this case translated from the Hebrew word, "**chatta**".[97] It means a criminal, or one accounted guilty, an offender, someone sinful, a sinner. The "scornful" is translated from the Hebrew word, "**luwts**"[98]   It means to make mouths at, to scoff, to mock, and to ridicule or have in derision.

---

[96] The New Strong's Exhaustive Concordance of the Bible, Hebrew Dictionary, page 135, word no 7563.
[97] The New Strong's Exhaustive Concordance of the Bible, Hebrew Dictionary, page 42, word no 2400.
[98] The New Strong's Exhaustive Concordance of the Bible, Hebrew Dictionary, page 69, word no 3887.

A believer who stays away from the company of those whose lives are described by Psalm 1:1 enjoys the blessings of God.

Ungodly company entangles you with the wicked making you a partaker of their sins.[99] The Bible has numerous accounts of people who missed the blessings of God and laboured under curses just because they associated with the ungodly. True repentance demanded that God's covenant people had to forsake their ungodly spouses.[100]

Please let no one think this verse is intended to promote divorces in churches. God hates divorce.[101] God has established authority in the Church.[102] What we bind on earth as servants of God, is bound in heaven.[103] When a man and a woman are bound and blessed in

---

[99] 2 John 9:16.
[100] Ezra 10:1–17.
[101] Malachi 2:16.
[102] Ephesians 4:11-13.
[103] Matthew 18:18–20.

Church and they consummate their marriage, they have become one in the sight of God. Therefore, what God has joined together, let not man put asunder.[104] The only Biblical ground one may stand upon for divorce is "fornication".[105]

A question has always been asked, "What if a Christian is married to a satanist who defies everything that is godly? One who demands that you do human sacrifices or that you become involved in homosexuality and other perversions? Well in such a case, you may have to choose between this ungodly marriage and the presence of God.[106] That is why it is not wise to marry a stranger. Pray before you make a decision about your marriage. There may be wisdom in taking counsel from godly, unselfish, married servants of God whose purpose is not to pull you down. Marriage as ordained by God is to be between male and female. The bride and groom should not wear 'masks' of pretence

---

[104] Matthew 19:3–6.
[105] Matthew 19:9.
[106] Psalm 1:1; 2 Corinthians 6:14–18.

before their wedding day. Let your spouse know your strong and weak points before the priest declares you husband and wife.

When a person associates with the wicked, not only is that person's character corrupted, he or she becomes a partaker of the sins of the wicked one. The would-be righteous person also partakes of the curses of his or her wicked associate.

There is wisdom in seeking to identify with the righteous.

Chapter 4.

Ungodly ties and covenants

A human being is a spirit, having a soul, living in a body. We are tri-une beings. Sometimes the word *"spirit"* and *"heart"* are used interchangeably in the scriptures to mean the same thing.[1] Your spirit or heart is the real you. That is the part of you which is born again when you commit your life to the Lordship of Jesus Christ.[2] That part of you becomes one with the Lord.[3] That is the part of you which worships God in spirit and in

---

[1] Psalm 13:5; Ezekiel 36:26–27; Luke 1:46-47.
[2] Ezekiel 36:26–29; 2 Corinthians 5:17; Ephesians 4:24; Colossians 3:9–10.
[3] 1 Corinthians 6:17.

truth.[4] That is the home of the fruit of the spirit.[5] For the ungodly it is the home for hatred and all other evil works of the flesh.[6]

Your soul comprises of your intellect, will and emotions. It is the part of you which reasons. The soul should be transformed by the Word of God.[7]

Your body is the house where you now live. It was formed out of the dust of the ground.[8] It is mortal.[9] Your body cannot inherit the kingdom of God.[10]

Ties exist in three realms. There are spirit ties, soul ties and bodily ties. Sometimes ties are ungodly and so bring about repercussions that are dangerous to the parties involved.

---

[4] John 4:24.
[5] Romans 5:5; Galatians 5:22–24.
[6] Mark 7:20–23.
[7] Romans 12:2; James 1:21.
[8] Genesis 2:7–8; Ecclesiastes 12:1–7.
[9] Romans 8:16.
[10] 1 Corinthians 15:50

A. SPIRIT TIES

These happen in the spirit realm. The Bible says when any person is joined to the Lord, he or she becomes ONE SPIRIT with Him.[11] Ananias and Sapphira opened a door for satan to work in their lives and so became one with the devil.[12] Every unbeliever has an evil spirit resident in their ungodly hearts. The scriptures tell us, it is *"the spirit that now worketh in the children of disobedience".*[13] They are dead spiritually and do not comprehend the counsel of God.[14]

Those who worship God in spirit and in truth have a spirit tie. They are spiritually tied together. They may not necessarily speak the same language. You may get any person from Uganda speaking Luganda, one from Egypt speaking Arabic, another from England speaking English or one from France whose language is French. Supposing each of them had no knowledge of any other language

---

[11] 1 Corinthians 6:7.
[12] Acts 5:1-3.
[13] Ephesians 2:1-3.
[14] 1 Corinthians 2:14.

except their own. If each of them loved and worshipped God in spirit and in truth, none of them may be lonely living with the rest of the group. They would have the fruit of the spirit.[15] They would be brethren. Why? They are spiritually tied together.

People who worship together having the same object of worship are spiritually tied together. For the children of God that spirit tie brings about righteousness, peace and joy in the Holy Ghost.[16] Those in the occult are also spiritually tied together. They have evil spirit ties. They are satanic ties. It takes the blood of Jesus Christ to break that bondage. Worshippers of satan have the same evil attitude regardless of their dialects or places of origin and residence. Why is it so? Well, they all have a satanic presence reigning in their hearts instead of the presence of God.[17]

The Word of God warns us against

---

[15] Galatians 5:22-23.
[16] Romans 14:17.
[17] Ephesians 2:1-3.

associating and fellowshipping with the wicked.[18] The priority on our agenda whenever we associate with them should be to win them to Christ.[19]

We worship the God of Abraham, Isaac and Jacob, the Father of our Lord Jesus Christ. Some people worship sports, others worship money, sex, power, fame, movies, stars, politicians, demons et cetera. Regardless of your object of worship, you will have a spirit tie with those who worship your way. Every form of perverted worship brings about loyalty to demonic spirits.[20] They enter into the victim's life and perpetuate their diabolic plans.

B. SOUL TIES.

Soul ties exist in the realm of intellect and emotions. There can be righteous soul ties in

---

[18] Psalm 1:1; 2 Corinthians 6:14-18.
[19] Matthew 28:19-20.
[20] Romans 6:16.

a situation like that of a church congregation, which has the same biblical mind.[21] A soul tie normally exists between a husband and wife. An emotional tie exists between a person and their object of influence. When you listen to someone or groups of people for some time, they are likely to affect your intellect, will and emotions.   The Bible warns us against ungodly company.[22]   Samson lost his anointing by listening to Delilah.[23]   You can always come across emotional captives of some politician, musician, actor, author, et cetera. No wonder Elijah destroyed the false prophets of his day.[24] That evil influence had to be wiped out of Israel.

Evil soul ties exist between people involved in ungodly relationships for example adultery, fornication, homosexuality, lesbianism, sexual orgies, pornography, or any other acts of sexual perversion involving two or more parties. By such relationships, demons are

---

[21] Romans 12:16; 1 Corinthians 1:10; Philippians 2:2.
[22] Psalm 1:1-2.
[23] Judges 16:1-20.
[24] 1 King 18:40.

easily transferred from one person to another. One easily becomes a partaker of the curses of his or her partner.[25]   In a sexual relationship, the two become one, in the spirit realm, in the realm of the soul and in the physical realm.[26] It takes total commitment to God for one to be delivered from the swarm of demons received during an orgasm with a demonized partner.

C. BODILY TIES:

Bodily ties exist between any two sexual partners.[27]   No wonder the Bible condemns adultery,[28] bestiality[29] and every other abusive use of our bodies.[30] When two bodies come together sexually, they do not only share each other's warmth and fluids, they share the diseases as well. HIV/AIDS and many other sexually transmitted diseases are easily

---

[25] Ezra 9 & 10.
[26] Genesis 2:23–24; Matthew 19:4–6; 1 Corinthians 6:16.
[27] Genesis 2:23–24; Matthew 19:4-6; 1 Corinthians 6:16.
[28] Exodus 20:14; Leviticus 20:10; Proverbs 6:7; Hebrews 13:4.
[29] Leviticus 18:23; 20:15-1.
[30] Leviticus 18:6-30; 20:10–21.

passed on from one sexual partner to another. What a painful day when one realizes they are troubled by a killer disease they got from an animal!

We live at a time when people almost make pets out of everything. You can have 'pet' lions, 'pet' wolves, 'pet' snakes, et cetera. I believe dogs, cats, pigs, horses and other animals should be loved and treated well,[31] but their place in life is surely neither at our dinning tables nor in our beds. I have also noticed that animals do not believe in Darwinism. They seem to believe once a predator, always a predator. Regardless of how long you keep them or even dress them up in human clothes calling them beautiful names, it takes less than a second for that beautiful lion, wolf or python to change from the cherished family pet to a dreadful predator dangerous to everyone in your household.

D. COVENANTS:

---

[31] Proverbs 12:10.

> 3. Can two walk together, except they be agreed?
>
> - Amos 3:3.

The Hebrew word for a covenant is **"beriyth"**.[32] It refers to a confederacy or a league. The Greek word for a covenant is **diatheke**.[33] It means a disposition or a contract especially a devisory will; a testament. The word covenant appears 285 times in the Hebrew Bible (first use at Genesis 6:18) and 33 times in the New Testament. God is a covenant keeping God.[34]

A covenant is an agreement or contract between two or more parties. Unlike a simple contract which refers to an exchange of goods and services, a covenant is more an exchange of persons; for example in a marriage, or when Israel is called God's *"firstborn son"* in Exodus 4:22. We also see

---

[32] The New Strong's Exhaustive Concordance of the Bible, Hebrew Dictionary, page 23, word no. 1285.
[33] The New Strong's Exhaustive Concordance of the Bible, Greek Dictionary, page 22, word no.1242.
[34] Exodus 2:24; Psalm 89:34.

reciprocity of relationship when God says: I will be your God, you will be my people.[35]

It is interesting to note that an agreement or a contract is founded upon mistrust. You sign an agreement or a contract with someone or a group of people and even call lawyers to bear witness of the transaction simply because neither party is willing to depend upon the spoken word of the other.

A covenant, on the contrary is built upon trust. You enter a covenant relationship with someone simply because you trust them enough to allow them be part of your life. So, there is greater intimacy in a covenant than there is in ordinary agreements and contracts.

Every human being is a spirit, having a soul, living in a physical body. The decisions that affect us are not initiated in the physical

---

[35] Exodus 6:7; Leviticus 26:12.

realm.[36] Covenants always involve a spirit being. They are anchored in the spirit realm.

A covenant revolves around four major pillars:

i. Terms and conditions;

ii. Promises and warnings;

iii. Responsibilities;

iv. Tokens, symbols and seals.

i. Terms and conditions:

Every covenant has terms and conditions which must be met by those who involve in it. For Abraham the terms were that he had to change his residence and lead his people to an unknown location which the Invisible God would show him.[37] He had to be a man with faith in God. Abraham had to recognize God as the Almighty God, to walk before Him and to be perfect.[38] For the Mosaic covenant

---

[36] Psalm 37:23, Jeremiah 10:23, Romans 8:14.
[37] Genesis 12:1.
[38] Genesis 17:1.

monotheism[39] and the Ten Commandments[40] were the terms. Any disregard of the oneness of God or of the Law was considered a violation of the covenant and would attract severe punishments.[41]

In the New Covenant by the blood of Jesus, of which we are beneficiaries, we are told there is only one Way through which any person can have access to God. That Way is through the Only Mediator; Jesus Christ.[42] Those are terms of the New Covenant. Any attempts to deal with God outside Christ are unacceptable.

ii. Promises and warnings:

In a covenant relationship there is always a promise of specific benefits, rewards, or blessings for people who keep the terms of the covenant; but they also threaten with sanctions, punishments, or curses for people

---

[39] Deuteronomy 6:4; Exodus 20:1-3
[40] Exodus 20:1-17, Deuteronomy 5:1-21
[41] John 8:1-5.
[42] John 14:6 Acts 4:12 and 1 Timothy 2:5-6

who break the terms of the covenant. In the Abrahamic covenant, there was a promise by God to make Abraham's descendants numerous,[43] to give him and his descendants land,[44] to make him and his offspring the only channel of blessing for all the nations of the earth.[45]

In the New Covenant we are promised a stress free eternal dwelling place with God.[46] We are also strongly warned about hell and the Lake of Fire.[47]

iii. Responsibilities:

Every covenant has responsibilities that go with it. God promised to bless Abraham but He also instructed him to "be a blessing".[48] The Mosaic covenant required Israel to fulfill all the responsibilities required by the Torah.[49]

---

[43] Genesis 12:2; 15:5; 17:20; 18:18.
[44] Genesis 12:1; 15:18-21; 17:8.
[45] Genesis 12:3; 18:18; 22:18; 26:4.
[46] John 14:1-3, 1 Thessalonians 4:13-17 and Revelation 21:1-7.
[47] Mark 9:43-48, Revelation 20:11-15 and 21:8
[48] Genesis 12:2.
[49] Joshua 1:8.

The Israelites were obliged to remember the statutes and judgments of God. They were to teach them to their children and children's children for as long as they lived.[50] In the New Covenant of which we are beneficiaries, we are commanded to go into all the world and preach the gospel to every creature.[51]

The parties involved in a covenant relationship might be individuals, families, nations, leaders, or even God. The parties might be on the same level. For example two families, two kings or any two ordinary people with mutual obligations agreed upon freely. Or they might be on different levels (God and humans; a large empire and a smaller nation) with the stronger party imposing the conditions on the weaker party (obedience, taxes, et cetera) in exchange for certain benefits.

For covenants made between humans (like

---

[50] Deuteronomy 4:1-9.
[51] Matthew 28:19-20; Mark 16:15.

the case of a holy marriage), both parties participate in establishing the rules and then invoke a higher spiritual authority (God) to oversee the agreement. In covenants made by God, the story is quite different. God works all the details out and He makes all the rules. God is Superior to humanity. Man is obliged to say "yes" to all the terms laid out. After a covenant is made, neither party is expected to violate it by virtue of the words, which were spoken the day it was made. Violation of a covenant is tantamount to treason. Not even God will dare to break his holy covenants.[52] No wonder God hates divorce.[53]

A covenant entitles you to the blessings, riches and other good things of your covenant partner. It also opens the door of your life for the curses, sorrows and other evils endured by your covenant partner to affect you. That is why one needs to be very careful before entering into a covenant relationship with anyone.

---

[52] Psalm 89:34.
[53] Malachi 2:16.

The covenant at Calvary entitled us to every good thing, which belongs to Jesus.[54]   It opened the door of His life for all our curses,[55] pains, iniquities, diseases, sorrows.[56] No wonder He was a man of sorrows acquitted with grief.[57]   He became sin that we might become the righteousness of God in Christ.[58]

iv.   Tokens, symbols and seals:

Covenants need to be ratified, many times sealed with blood, and thus often involve animal sacrifices.   In a covenant relationship there are concrete tokens, symbols or *"signs"* that are often exchanged to remind the two parties about their agreement.   In the Noahic covenant, we have the rainbow to remind us that the waters shall no more become a flood to destroy all flesh.[59]   In the Abrahamic covenant it is the circumcision of all

---

[54] Ephesians 1:3; 2 Peter 1:3.
[55] Galatians 3:13-14.
[56] Isaiah 53:3-6; Matthew 8:17.
[57] Isaiah 53:3.
[58] 2 Corinthians 5:21.
[59] Genesis 9:8-17.

Abraham's male descendants.[60]   In the Mosaic covenant the stone tablets were a token.

In the New Covenant we are sealed with the Holy Spirit of Promise.[61]

E.   BLOOD COVENANTS

For every covenant there are words spoken. Vows are exchanged and a patron or a higher spirit power is invoked to see to it that neither party violates the terms agreed upon. At times, these covenants involve the shedding of blood.

In many of the pre-Christian African societies if two men came together, each of them would cut his navel, smear his blood on a coffee bean, exchange it with his colleague, and

---

[60] Genesis 17:9-14, 23-27; 21:4.
[61] Ephesians 1:13.

each of the two would eat his colleague's blood-soaked coffee bean. They would become blood covenant brothers. A satanic priest would declare abundant benefits which each of them would enjoy if they remained faithful to the terms of the covenant. He would also pronounce some curses, which would come upon any, or both of the parties involved if they dared to violate the covenant. By virtue of this covenant relationship a person would share the blessings of their new brother or sister. Denying your covenant brother or sister the safety, protection or provisions they needed from you would be a violation of the covenant. Yet none would be expected to take advantage of the other selfishly.

Every covenant breaker would open his life to the curses pronounced the day that covenant was ratified. Whoever honoured the covenant would enjoy the blessings contained in the covenant package.

A person's descendants were also obliged to keep the covenants established by him or his ancestors. God judges people who get involved in ungodly covenants.[62] It is therefore possible for a person to endure curses just because his or her ancestors were part of an evil covenant!

F.   EVIL SEXUAL COVENANTS.

These affect the three parts of a human being. Our Lord Jesus warned us against committing adultery in our hearts and in our minds.[63]

Sexual covenants involve a person's heart, soul, and flesh. There is a spirit tie, a soul tie and finally a bodily tie.

Sometimes there is a spilling of blood. For instance in the case of (yet not limited to)

---

[62] Ezra 9-10; Hebrews 13:4.
[63] Matthew 5:27-30.

broken virginity. Sometimes tokens are exchanged. They may be tangible or intangible. They may be names. There may be words spoken by either party before, during, or after the sexual act. Some of these words may be vows. For example, *"I will always love you until the Nile and the Mediterranean dry up"* or *"Let heaven and earth record that I will never have another partner all the days of my life".*

Some of those confessions are of course foolish and uncalled for. Yet the spirit world acknowledges their validity. Behind these immoral practices normally lies very strong evil spirits of sexual perversion, which would ensure that such a covenant is not broken. Therefore, a young woman may fail to get married just because of a promise she made to a man during sexual intercourse; *"I will never leave you until all the oceans dry up!"* The two may be living separate lives but the sexual covenant they entered into still affects them because the oceans have not dried up yet. They are ensnared by the words of their mouths.[64]

An evil sexual covenant opens your life not only to every curse and contagious disease suffered by your partner but also to the influence of demons which may lead you to grosser sexual perversions. You become lustful.

Many times demons cling to people and places because of covenants. Covenants are agreements. Once there is an agreement of any kind with the powers of darkness, they will not hesitate to exploit that opportunity to cling to that person's life. Well, *"Can two walk together, except they be agreed?"* - Amos 3:3.

It takes the blood of Jesus, the Word of God and the anointing of the Holy Spirit to break such strong evil covenants!

When I committed my life to the Lordship of

---

[64] Proverbs 6:2

Jesus Christ the Son of God, I knew I had taken a bold step to come out of the kingdom of darkness. I verbally renounced the evil covenants and embraced the New Covenant of the blood of Jesus. However, I still honoured a few tokens and responsibilities from prince of this world because alcohol remained a great friend to me. My excuse was always 1 Timothy 5:23, *"Drink no longer water, but use a little wine for thy stomach's sake and thine often infirmities"*. I still drank *"a little"* supposedly for my *"stomach's sake"* and *"my often infirmities"* despite the fact that I had no stomach problems and that no medical doctor had ever prescribed alcohol as a drug for me. I was convinced I loved the Lord Jesus, yet I still treasured the ways of the world.

It was not uncommon for me to spend some days in prayer and fasting only to break my fast with a few beers. Every plan to discourage me was futile because I loved my bondage. Obviously, the more I defended my drinking habits the more enslaved to alcohol I realized I was.

While intoxicated, I would sometimes grin and shout, *"Alcohol, mwenge,*[65] *the loved enemy"!* There were also times when I would console myself by quoting names of religious men and women who I knew to be drunkards as well.

It is sad to live in bondage. It is more pathetic when a prisoner accepts his bondage morally and spiritually. Worse still if they prisoner cherishes and celebrates their bondage with great rejoicing.

In 1989 Apostle Evans Mrima of Gospel Outreach, Ngara hosted us to a conference at Kenyatta International Conference Centre (KICC) in Nairobi, Kenya. It was about power evangelism. Delegates came from a number of African countries, Europe, Asia and the United States of America. I did not check into a hotel. I chose to spend that week with my cousins who were Muslims.

---

[65] Mwenge is the Luganda word for alcohol.

One night after a very great move of God I returned home and asked my Muslim cousins to accompany me to a drinking pub so I would buy myself some beers. They tried to restrain me but I quoted 1 Timothy 5:23 and argued my way out. So, off we went. The Muslims stayed outside the pub. I, the man of God entered, went straight to the counter and placed my order. I bought myself some two bottles of *"Guinness for Power"* and drank from my bedroom.

That night I had a dream when I was swimming in a sewage tank. All my body was covered with a mixture of rotten stinking human excreta. I abhorred the dream. I felt like vomiting.

All I could think about was 2 Peter 2:22, *"The dog is turned to his own vomit again; and the sow that was washed to her wallowing in the mire".* I felt so remorseful when I thought about the price Jesus paid for my redemption and how I had abused His grace. I imagined how many of my Muslim relatives I had discouraged from receiving Christ as their Lord and Savior just because of my lack of self control. I thought about the danger of standing before God one day to give an account for all the careless words I spoke and the careless actions I was responsible for when under the influence of alcohol.[66]

The Bible says, *"Whether therefore ye eat, or drink, or whatsoever ye do, do all to the glory of God" - 1 Corinthians 10:31.* Was I surely drinking for the glory of God? Obviously, **NO**. I knew I was in trouble. I repented and asked God to take that ungodly desire away from me. I made a vow never to drink alcohol again for as long as I live.

Since 1989 alcohol and I have never been friends again and in Jesus' Name we will never be friends again for as long as both of us shall live on this planet. I also made an irrevocable decision to renounce all evil tokens and responsibilities pertaining to the

---

[66] Matthew 12:36-37.

kingdom of darkness from where God's grace saved me.

It is ungodly to come out of the kingdom of darkness and yet keep treasuring its promises, tokens and responsibilities. I have met some Christians whose lives remained miserable just because the still held on to gifts from their ex-lovers or because of some tokens from a sorcerer which they received while in the world.

In the name of souvenirs some people have accursed things in their houses.[67] Others struggle with certain bondages because they still do satan's assignments; they treasure fornication, lies, theft, and other ungodly habits while pretending to belong to Jesus. The devil regards those as areas of agreement with him and always tries his best to follow them up.[68]

---

[67] Deuteronomy 7:25-26
[68] Amos 3:3.

All the four pillars of the evil covenants should be permanently broken. We should embrace all the pillars of the New Covenant by the blood of Jesus. Let heaven, earth and hell know where we stand concerning our commitment to God.

Beloved, my problem was alcohol. What is yours? Such ungodly responsibilities hinder a person from enjoying the blessings of the New Covenant. The Bible tells us to *"Abstain from all appearance of evil"*.[69] The Lord Jesus said, *"The prince of this world ... hath nothing in Me"*.[70] We need to be in a position to make such a statement meaning it from the bottom of our hearts.

---

[69] 1 Thessalonians 5:22.
[70] John 14:30.

Chapter 5.

The four point program of a curse

Curses have a programme by which they operate. The result is destruction of their prey. Their programme is well spelt out in Deuteronomy 28:45.

> 45. Moreover all these curses shall come upon thee, and shall pursue thee, and overtake thee, till thou be destroyed; because thou hearkenedst not unto the voice of

the LORD thy God, to keep His
commandments and His statutes
which He commanded thee.

- Deuteronomy 28:45.

Curses have a four point programme
according to Deuteronomy 28:45. They come
upon, they pursue, they overtake, and they
finally destroy their victims.

(a). They come upon:

The Bible declares, "Curses shall come upon"
those who disregard the counsel of God.[1]

This means that curses do "impose
themselves upon" their victims. One does not
have to be interested in them or may not even
have knowledge about them. As long as you
fall prey to them, curses come upon you.
They impose themselves upon you
dominating and controlling your life and

---

[1] Deuteronomy 28:45.

everything which matters to you so that nothing ever works out in your favour. They take advantage of you and rob you of your time, strength, joy, resources, and so much more.

Sighing, crying or suicide cannot stop the power of a curses from tormenting a family. You need the hand of God.

(b). They pursue:

The second thing curses do after they come upon a victim is to pursue him or her. The Hebrew word from which "pursue" is translated in Deuteronomy 28:45 is "**radaph**".[2] It means to run after (usually with hostile intent), to chase, put to flight, follow (after, an), hunt or persecute. That is exactly what curses do in the lives of their victims.

A curse pursues its victim with an intension to disgrace and destroy them. Many times the

---

[2] The New Strong's Exhaustive Concordance of the Bible, Hebrew Dictionary, Page 130, word no. 7291.

victim may do everything within his or her power to try and flee from this invisible force working against them. One may change their profession, address, accent, complexion, or even their dress code. None of these helps.

A curse cannot be broken by the geography or economy of your residence. It is a spiritual problem. It requires a spiritual solution!

(c). They overtake:

Curses operate in the spirit realm before they are manifested in the physical realm. Because they are spiritual, they move faster than any physical being. A person who labours under a curse may travel by the fastest means available from one location to another only to find the same problems he fled from awaiting him at his destination. A curse does not allow that person's change of address to become a reason for victory!

You happen to be interviewed for a job, for which you are well qualified only to seem as though someone went ahead of you and turned the hearts of the interviewers against you. Why? A curse overtook you!

You wonder why so and so suffers the same problems regardless of the country or continent they move to. Curses came upon them; they pursued them relentlessly, and overtook them! A curse overwhelms and overshadows its victim!

(d). They destroy:

The fourth and final point as far as curses are concerned is destruction. Just like devil, curses come *"to steal and to kill, and to destroy".*[3] Curses operate strategically. They use three major tactics to achieve their goal:

i. Laying siege;

ii. Causing cycles of defeat;

iii. Adversity.

---

[3] John 10:10.

Every manifestation of curses comes under this strategy, and the end result of the strategy is destruction.

i.   CURSES BESIEGE.

> 52. And he shall besiege thee in all thy gates, until thy high and fenced walls come down, wherein thou trustedst, throughout all thy land: and he shall besiege thee in all thy gates throughout all thy land, which the LORD thy God hath given thee
>
> - Deuteronomy 28:52.

I was born and raised in Uganda. We experienced so many turbulent times as a country. Different leaders have come to power because of the gun and gone out of office the same way. The world has known about Field Marshal Idi Amin Dada and some of the regimes that followed his. Sometimes people ask me what it was like to live under Idi Amin's tyranny with no freedom of speech. Well, I was a little boy but the joke that goes with it is that Uganda has never had a time where there was no freedom of speech. We always had the liberty to say whatever we wanted to say during Idi Amin's time. All we never had was freedom after the speech. So we stayed silent, wincing with pain as gruesome murders by state organs became the trend of the day. The painful truth is that Idi Amin was not Uganda's worst nightmare. Some of the *'heroes'* who *'liberated'* us from his tyranny committed worse atrocities.

During one of Uganda's armed conflicts, there was an incident when the enemy force; Yoweri Museveni's National Resistance Army at that time, surrounded an army barracks in the southern part of Uganda (Kasijjagirwa; Masaka). The soldiers in the barracks could not get any help from outside their fence. Everything they trusted in ceased to be helpful because the enemy had surrounded them. They were captives in a land supposed to be under their control. Their lives were at the mercy of their enemies. Finally, they surrendered to their enemies. The barracks was overrun. That is the way a curse operates.

A curse besieges its victims. Someone under a curse is besieged. No matter what he or she does trying to escape or hide from the enemy, nothing seems to be of help. All their *"high and fenced walls come down"*[4] because they cannot stand the pressure mounted by the armed forces against them. It is a slow but sure tormenting, sorrowful, painful death. One literally feels the hand of death looming over their lives.

These *"high and fenced walls"* may be anything a person trusts in for security, protection or a prestigious identity. It may be a carrier, money, friends, reputation, education, physical strength, talents and abilities, political privileges, ministry, et cetera. Whatever the walls are, they can come down under the siege of a curse! Such should have been the frustration of Jericho's inhabitants when the Israelites besieged their city.[5] Their walls finally collapsed and they were helpless in the presence of their enemies!

---

[4] Deuteronomy 28:52.
[5] Joshua 6:1-24.

ii.   CYCLES OF DEFEAT:

It is very interesting to see a cycle or a wheel turning. No part of it can stay on top all the time because it keeps on turning as time and distance go unnoticed. At one time "**point A**" of the cycle or wheel is up while "**point S**" is down. Then all of a sudden "**point S**" comes on top and "**point A**" realizes the victory was short lived.

It is also a painful reality when one looks at a cycle in its horizontal position spinning around.   Or in its vertical position but suspended from the ground. However fast the cycle moves, time and energy will remain wasted without any distance being covered because a force that will not allow it to touch the ground controls it.   In such a case you have motion without progress.

Curses bring about a cycle of defeat in the life of a person, family, or society. Think about an individual who works so hard yet his efforts are frustrated every time he gets to the last minute. That is what a curse does! Think

97

about a recurring nightmare! That is how a curse torments! Think about a good, harmless person who tries his or her best to live a victorious life. Every time this person seems to have some peace, quiet and rest or joy, the monster of fear, failure and trauma shows up. Their happiness is short lived. It is pseudo-victory.

There is a game called snakes and ladders. You throw a dice, score a six and that starts you off. You keep moving from "**0**" towards "**100**" depending on your scores. Sometimes your score leads you to a ladder and your progress is speeded up. There are times when your score lands you to the mouth of a serpent. It is then assumed that you have been bitten by that serpent and so you have to move backwards till you settle where its tail ends. It is a very frustrating experience if every time you get to your seventies, eighties, or nineties the snakebite takes your back to the initial stages of the game. That is how a curse operates!

It is as if some diabolic being lurking in the dark pounces upon this individual or family every time a smile comes their way. Wages and salaries seem to be planned for by some invisible enemy.[6] Life becomes traumatic, characterized by calamity after calamity. One becomes acquainted with grief and sorrow.

iii.   ADVERSITY.

A third way, by means of which curses destroy their victims, is by ushering times of adversity into the victims' lives and programmes.

Adversity in life, endless struggles, fruitless groaning and travailing all the time, ups and downs, calamities, ill luck, being a scapegoat or a perpetual loser. No matter what a person does, things seem to grow from bad to worse all the time. In some cases, one may be tempted to believe prayer is meaningless. Heaven and earth seem unfriendly to this person. One sees themselves as a victim of circumstances.   The Bible describes this

---

[6] Haggai 1:6.

painful state in a number of ways, yet I believe these two verses paint the best picture about adversity:

> 20. The LORD shall send upon thee cursing, vexation, and rebuke, in all that thou settest thine hand unto for to do, until thou be destroyed and until thou perish quickly; because of the wickedness of thy doings whereby thou hast forsaken Me.
>
> 23. And thy heaven that is over thy head shall be brass, and the earth that is under thee shall be iron.
>
> - Deuteronomy 28:20, 23.

The ultimate goal of a curse is destruction. Just like the devil, the curse is a thief who comes only to kill, steal, and destroy.[7]

---

[7] John 10:10.

Chapter 6.

The story of Cain

1. And Adam knew Eve his wife; and she conceived, and bare Cain, and said, I have gotten a man from the LORD.

2. And she again bare his brother Abel. And Abel was a keeper of sheep, but Cain was a tiller of the ground.

3.   And in process of time it came to pass, that Cain brought of the fruit of the ground an offering unto the LORD.

4.   And Abel, he also brought of the firstlings of his flock and of the fat thereof. And the LORD had respect unto Abel and to his offering:

5.   But unto Cain and to his offering he had not respect. And Cain was very wroth, and his countenance fell.

6.   And the LORD said unto Cain, Why art thou wroth? and why is thy countenance fallen?

7.   If thou doest well, shalt thou not be accepted? and if thou doest

not well, sin lieth at the door. And unto thee *shall be* his desire, and thou shalt rule over him.

8.　　And Cain talked with Abel his brother: and it came to pass, when they were in the field, that Cain rose up against Abel his brother, and slew him.

9.　　And the LORD said unto Cain, Where *is* Abel thy brother? And he said, I know not: *Am* I my brother's keeper?

10.　　And he said, What hast thou done? the voice of thy brother's blood crieth unto me from the ground.

11.　　And now *art* thou cursed from the earth, which hath opened her mouth to receive thy brother's blood from thy hand;

12.　　When thou tillest the ground, it shall not henceforth yield unto thee her strength; a fugitive and a vagabond shalt thou be in the earth.

13.　　And Cain said unto the LORD, My punishment *is* greater than I can bear.

14.　　Behold, thou hast driven me out this day from the face of the earth; and from thy face shall I be hid; and I shall be a fugitive and a vagabond in the earth; and it shall come to pass, *that* every one that findeth me shall slay me.

15.   And the LORD said unto him, Therefore whosoever slayeth Cain, vengeance shall be taken on him sevenfold. And the LORD set a mark upon Cain, lest any finding him should kill him.

16.   And Cain went out from the presence of the LORD, and dwelt in the land of Nod, on the east of Eden.

17.   And Cain knew his wife; and she conceived, and bare Enoch: and he builded a city, and called the name of the city, after the name of his son, Enoch.

18.   And unto Enoch was born Irad: and Irad begat Mehujael: and Mehujael begat Methusael: and Methusael begat Lamech.

19.   And Lamech took unto him two wives: the name of the one *was* Adah, and the name of the other Zillah.

23.   And Lamech said unto his wives, Adah and Zillah, Hear my voice; ye wives of Lamech, hearken unto my speech: for I have slain a man to my wounding, and a young man to my hurt.

24.   If Cain shall be avenged sevenfold, truly Lamech seventy and sevenfold.

- Genesis 4:1-19, 23-24.

The first two verses of Genesis chapters four show us their mother conceived once and gave birth twice, an indication that Cain and Abel were twins.   The two boys grew up together as members of one family.

"In the process of time, it came to pass, that" each of the boys brought an offering to the LORD. Cain brought an offering of the fruit of the ground "unto the LORD". Abel brought an offering "of the firstling of his flock and of the fat thereof" to the LORD. Abel found favour before God. God rejected Cain and his offering. Cain was very displeased and his countenance fell. That is common with many people whose deliberate sin denies them access the blessings of God.

The seventh verse reveals something we need to take note of; *"If thou doest well, shall thou not be accepted"?* These two knew what was right. When their parents transgressed the commandment of the LORD in the Garden of Eden, they tried to cover the shame of their nakedness by dressing up in leaves. That could only bless for a while.

Later on God made for them coats of skins. Where were these skins from unless some animal had been slaughtered in garden? It is evident that Adam and Eve told their descendants about the importance of animal blood until the seed of the woman, Jesus of Nazareth would bruise the head of the serpent. They should also have told these two about the curse upon the ground. Hebrews 11:4 later confirms this truth; *"By faith Abel offered unto God a more excellent sacrifice than Cain".* How does faith come? It comes by hearing.[1] Therefore, they had heard. Or else how would God hold them accountable? (Please get my book; "Now Faith Is")

It is therefore evident that Cain knew what to do but chose to disregard the revealed truth of his time.

Then he shed innocent human blood by slaying his brother! God told him there was a curse from the earth upon his life as a result of his sin. It is very important for us to observe how this curse operated.

---

[1] Romans 10:17.

10.   And he said, What hast thou done? the voice of thy brother's blood crieth unto me from the ground.

11.   And now *art* thou cursed from the earth, which hath opened her mouth to receive thy brother's blood from thy hand;

12.   When thou tillest the ground, it shall not henceforth yield unto thee her strength; a fugitive and a vagabond shalt thou be in the earth.

13.   And Cain said unto the LORD, My punishment *is* greater than I can bear.

14.   Behold, thou hast driven me out this day from the face of the

earth; and from thy face shall I be hid; and I shall be a fugitive and a vagabond in the earth; and it shall come to pass, *that* every one that findeth me shall slay me.

15.   And the LORD said unto him, Therefore whosoever slayeth Cain, vengeance shall be taken on him sevenfold. And the LORD set a mark upon Cain, lest any finding him should kill him.

16.   And Cain went out from the presence of the LORD, and dwelt in the land of Nod, on the east of Eden.

- Genesis 4:10-16.

God rejected Cain. He became an example of how devastating the curse of a vagabond can be in the life of a person. We read in verse 12: *"When thou tillest the ground ..."*. God did not stop Cain from tilling the ground or investing his resources, time and abilities in any business or agricultural project. God did not say, *"If thou tillest the ground ..."*. He said, *"When thou tillest the ground ..."*. It wasn't "**IF**". It was "**WHEN**". Cain was expected to *"till the ground"*. Yet he would never live to see the earth yield her strength to him. In our modern day, he would perhaps have access to all the necessary agricultural personnel, tools, and fertilizers. His farm would perhaps start as the best on the planet.

It is interesting to note that at such a time Cain should have been considered a very privileged young man. His family had access to almost everything on the planet; lands, animals, birds, fishes, jewels, rivers, oceans, et cetera. He went to the best *'University'* of his time because *'Professor'* Adam who taught him named everything. Abel had died so he was now an only son. His father was committed to only one wife; no girlfriends, no concubines. They did not any evil neighbours. The visitor their home knew was God Himself. Yet all his endeavours would only bring him tears because he lacked the major ingredient in all his plans, *"the blessing of the LORD"* which *"maketh rich and addeth no sorrow"* – Proverbs 10:22.

Cain became a *"fugitive and a vagabond"* – a homeless wonderer. Perhaps he would start some very well-planned project off in one location of the planet. Regardless of how hard he worked, he would only seem like one who has engaged a reverse gear.

For a person like Cain earth and every natural factor seems not to be in their favour. So they always move from one location to another expecting things to work better at the new address. After investing so heavily in the new location, more disappointments come their way; thieves, natural hazards, or the ground just proves infertile. Then they would move on, and on, and on.

Cain would shift to another location only to find out that the geography, history, and economy of his new place were not a remedy. Either the neighbours were unfriendly or he would find himself haunted by the guilt of having murdered his brother. Perhaps his sleep was always characterized with nightmares. Such things always happen to those who shed innocent human blood! Frustration became his portion.

The curse brought him sorrow of heart. He went on the defensive attempting to send the Holy One on a guilt trip. There is a tendency for people laboring under a curse to feel they have been punished beyond what they deserve for their sins.

13. And Cain said unto the LORD, My punishment *is* greater than I can bear.

14. Behold, thou hast driven me out this day from the face of the earth; and from thy face shall I be hid; and I shall be a fugitive and a

vagabond in the earth; and it shall come to pass, *that* every one that findeth me shall slay me.

- Genesis 4:13-14.

Fear and sorrow become the portion of those who experience this type of a curse. Sorrowful moments always create an opportunity for demons to enter and inhabit the life of an individual. *"Fear hath torment"* – 1 John 4:18. (We will share more about this later in the following chapter: "**Curses and demons**").

Cain should have felt haunted and pursued all the time, everywhere! Life became a recurring nightmare! He told God, *"Behold, thou hast driven me out this day from the face of the earth"* – Genesis 4:14. No place on earth would serve as a home for him any longer. Have you observed the life of a murderer before? Perhaps you have seen those guilty of shedding innocent human blood by abortion or their descendants. We will share more about this later on.

Cain could not access the presence of God. He said; *"and from thy face shall I be hid"* – Genesis 4:12. He became a stranger to the presence of God. Have you ever wondered why some people pray, fast and do all sorts of things to capture the attention of God yet their lives do not bear much evidence of God's anointing?[2] Perhaps they need to repent for some innocent human blood they or their ancestors shed![3] God visits "the iniquity of the fathers upon the children unto the third and fourth generation" - Exodus 20:5.

The favour of God departed from Cain's life. He became a candidate of no favour and no mercy before humanity and circumstances. He said, *"and I shall be a fugitive and a vagabond in the earth; and it shall come to pass, that every one that findeth me shall slay me".[4]* As far as Cain was concerned, everyone had become an enemy! Have you met people in life who go telling stories of how everyone is after them and how everyone

---

[2] Isaiah 58:1–5.
[3] Isaiah 59:1–8.
[4] Genesis 4:12.

seeks to kill them? In some cases, they may have a point but many times all that such people need is sincerity and a restoration of their fellowship with God! It starts when we confess and forsake our sins. True repentance has never meant anything less.[5] That was what Cain needed!

The curse of a vagabond shortens a person's lifespan *"every one that findeth me shall slay me"* - Genesis 4:12.

This moment became a turning point in Cain's life. It brought about sorrow in his heart and opened the door of his life for a raging spirit as we see later on in Genesis 4:23.

He became an enemy of those who appeared successful! Frustration can build resentment in a person's heart against all those he regards successful. Later on, Cain attempts to kill one of his descendants. Lamech being younger overpowers him and slays him. That

[5] Proverb 28:13; Isaiah 55:7.

is when we realize Cain's problem was no longer limited to him alone. It was now in the family. His offspring had inherited the evil spirit. The curse was inherited by generations after him.

There was need for someone to break this curse from the bloodline. That person would have to start with repentance.

> 23. And Lamech said unto his wives, Adah and Zillah, Hear my voice; ye wives of Lamech, hearken unto my speech: for I have slain a man to my wounding, and a young man to my hurt.

> 24. If Cain shall be avenged sevenfold, truly Lamech seventy and sevenfold.

> - Genesis 4:23-24.

If anyone thought Cain was a problem, they would not have to wait long before seeing the grosser vices Lamech and his descendants were capable of displaying on the stage of human history!

Chapter 7.

Curses and demons

We have defined curses. We need to know what demons are and some of their characteristics mentioned in the written Word of God. demons are evil spirits. demons serve the interest of satan against God's creation. They are persons without physical bodies.

43. When the unclean spirit is gone out of a man, he walketh through dry places, seeking rest, and findeth none.

44.   Then he saith, I will return into my house from whence I came out; and when he is come, he findeth *it* empty,   swept,   and garnished.

45.   Then goeth he, and taketh with himself seven other spirits more wicked than himself, and they enter in and dwell there: and the last *state* of that man is worse than the first. Even so shall it be also unto this wicked generation.

- Matthew 12:43-45.

From the verses of Scripture we have just quoted, we learn some important truths about evil spirits *(interchangeably referred to as demons).*

1.   They are persons without physical bodies.

2.   They are unclean (See also Matthew 10:1; Mark 1:23).

3.   They think and make decisions.

4.   They can think and express themselves.

5. They have different ranks and varying degrees of wickedness.

6. They have knowledge, skills and desires.

7. They grow weary (that is why they seek a place of rest).

8. They seek to inhabit flesh and blood. They obsess and finally oppress their victims - (see Mark 5:1-13 & Acts 16:16).

9. They regard themselves soldiers and can work in groups, legions or battalions subject to one leader - verse 45 (see also Mark 5:8-9).

10. They are persistent. Once cast out of an individual they become nostalgic and very desperate. That is why they always seek to return to a *"house"* they once lost.

There is more information about demons in other portions of scripture.

11. They believe in God – James 2:19.

12. Their knowledge of God causes them to tremble – James 2:19.

13. They serve satan's interests - Matthew 12:26.

14. They are numerous – Mark 5:9.

15. They seek to inhabit and control people and animals - Mark 5:13; Acts 16:16.

16. They can cause emotional, mental and physical problems and infirmities – Matthew 12:22; Mark 5:4-5; Luke 13:11-16.

17. They can afflict with sicknesses and diseases - Job 2:7-8, Matthew 17:14-15; Acts 10:38.

18. Some demonic problems can be masquerade as medical challenges – Job 2:7-8.

19. They can cling to territories and objects – Mark 5:8-10; Acts 16:18-19.

20. We do not have to know their specific names because they can be identified and

named after their activities. For example, there are deaf, dumb, and blind spirits - Matthew 12:22; Mark 9:17, 25; Luke 11:14; 12:22.

21. They are ferocious and extremely and destructive – Matthew 8:28.

22. They torment and exasperate their captives – Luke 6:18.

23. They entice, coerce and lead people into sin – Luke 4:1-13; Revelation 16:13-14.

24. They try to deceive believers – Ephesians 6:11-12; 1 Timothy 4:1-2.

25. They appear religious at times, have doctrines, and are the founders of cults and every perverted form of worship – 1 Timothy 4:1–3.

26. They hate holy marriages blessed by God's servants – 1 Timothy 4:3.

27. They can manifest themselves through leaders and systems of governance – 1 Samuel 16:14-23; 18:10-11; Revelation 16:14.

28. They know the Lord Jesus Christ, recognize His authority and are subject to His Lordship of Jesus and His Name – Matthew 4:24; 8:16, 28–29; Mark 16:17; Luke 10:17; Acts 19:13-15; James 2:19.

29. Believers have authority over demons and should always cast them out in the Name of Jesus – Mark 16:17; Luke 10:17; Acts 8:5–8; 16:17; 1 John 4:4.

30. They know the difference between anointed servants of God and imposters – Acts 19:11-16.

31. They were defeated and disarmed by the Lord Jesus Christ at Calvary – Colossians 2:15.

32. They serve an eternally defeated leader; satan - Hebrews 2:14.

33. They are part of a kingdom declining to its end – 1 Corinthians 2:6.

34. They have an imminent terrible eternal destiny – Matthew 25:41.

35. They know their end – Matthew 8:29; Luke 8:31.

Because evil spirits are hungry for flesh and blood, they seek to exploit any given opportunity to enter into the life of a person or bloodline to perpetuate their diabolic plans. Sin subjects a person to satan's power[1] and thus serves as a door for demons to enter into his or her life. The Bible warns us against satan's snares. They are always found along three avenues: the lust of the flesh, the lust of the eyes and the pride of life. Any of these can serve as an entrance for demons into someone's life.

> 15. Love not the world, neither the things *that are* in the world. If any man love the world, the love of the Father is not in him.

> 16. For all that *is* in the world, the lust of the flesh, and the lust of the eyes, and the pride of life, is not of the Father, but is of the world.

---

[1] Genesis 4:6–8; Romans 6:12-14.

17. And the world passeth away, and the lust thereof: but he that doeth the will of God abideth for ever.

- 1 John 2:15-17.

Fear or any traumatic experience can also be a great opportunity for demons to enter into the life of a person or the lives of a group of people. *"Fear hath torment"* – 1 John 4:18.

The joy of the LORD is our strength.[2] Without His joy we are weak. Curses bring about sorrow in a person's heart. Therefore, curses serve to open the door of a person's life for demons to enter therein and affect that individual and his descendants or subjects. That is why some people do not obtain their deliverance until the curses they labour under have been broken. It does not matter how many deliverance sessions a person goes through, if the curses are not broken, the door

---

[2] Nehemiah 8:10c.

of that person's life will remain open and accessible to demonic spirits.

Living in sin is like digging a pit for oneself, or breaking one's hedge of protection against demonic forces.   Sin brings about curses. Curses attract demons.   demons ruin and destroy the life of their victims.

> 8.   He that diggeth a pit shall fall into it, and whoso breaketh an hedge, a serpent shall bite him.
>
> - Ecclesiastes 10:8.

In this case a serpent is symbolic of demonic powers. demonic spirits are so opportunistic they would seek to exploit every door opened to them.

Therefore, we always need to start by dealing with the sin issue. There is always a need for repentance and a renunciation of evil covenants before breaking curses. Once curses are broken then demonic activity can easily be stopped.

Chapter 8.

Twelve indicators of a curse

It is easy to notice a curse operating in the life of a person, a family, a bloodline or society by observing its effects in the life of that person, family, bloodline or society.

There are a number of signs which may indicate the operation of a curse in someone's life. Sometimes we have taken so many things for granted and failed to seek the help we need in certain areas. We have pretended to live as though nothing is wrong with us. We have chosen to walk the broad, shining, yet slippery way of pretence leading to destruction when the seemingly shameful narrow path of truth would have saved us![1]

Again, some dear saints end up demonizing everything. Such brethren choose to *"see"* a demon in every name, place, object, friend, enemy, et cetera. They paint a picture of an invincible, mighty, wicked devil whose authority and influence has no limits. That too is a fallacy!

Something ought to be re-emphasized. It is not as important to know the size and shape of the devil, as it is to know Christ. It is not as important to understand curses, as it is to understand God's blessings. However, we cannot choose to be ignorant of our enemy's devices because that would give the enemy a great advantage over us.

---

[1] Matthew 7:13-14.

11. Lest satan should get an advantage of us: for we are not ignorant of his devices.

- 2 Corinthians 2:11.

1. Endless unnecessary financial problems

It is not unheard of for the righteous to face financial challenges for a moment in life. Many are the challenges, which we encounter in life, but God causes us to triumph in every one of them. The Bible says:

19. Many *are* the afflictions of the righteous: but the LORD delivereth him out of them all.

- Psalm 34:19.

That is not a calling to poverty. Lack is not our portion.

25.   I   have   been   young, and *now* am   old;   yet   have   I   not seen   the   righteous   forsaken,   nor his seed begging bread.

26.   *He*   *is* ever   merciful,   and lendeth; and his seed *is* blessed.

- Psalm 37:25-26.

By virtue of our place in Christ Jesus, we are blessed.[2]

3.   Blessed *be* the   God   and Father   of   our   Lord   Jesus   Christ, who   hath   blessed   us   with   all spiritual   blessings   in heavenly *places* in Christ:

- Ephesians 1:3.

---

[2] Galatians 3:13-14; Ephesians 1:3; 2 Peter 1:2-4.

9.   For ye know the grace of our Lord Jesus Christ, that, though he was rich, yet for your sakes he became poor, that ye through his poverty might be rich.

- 2 Corinthians 8:9.

1.   Blessed *is* the man that walketh not in the counsel of the ungodly, nor standeth in the way of sinners, nor sitteth in the seat of the scornful.

2.   But his delight *is* in the law of the LORD; and in his law doth he meditate day and night.

3.   And he shall be like a tree planted by the rivers of water, that bringeth forth his fruit in his season; his leaf also shall not wither; and whatsoever he doeth shall prosper.

- Psalm 1:1-3.

Then why do some of God's children lack and suffer hunger? Why do some of them labour under heavy spiritual burdens and yokes of bondage?

Well, some go through these unnecessary pains because of laziness, ignorance, or rebellion against the counsel of God. The reasons are diverse. In this book, we will talk more about those who cannot prosper because of curses.

Recalling the story of Cain in the fourth chapter of Genesis, we observe that he could till the ground and invest. No one stopped him from planning and labouring. He still had all his God given wisdom and strength but he was denied the joy of ever having a harvest.[3] Why? There was a curse upon his life due to the innocent human blood which he shed.[4]

> 4. Ye have sown much, and bring in little; ye eat, but ye have

---

[3] Genesis 4:12.
[4] Genesis 4:1-16.

not enough; ye drink, but ye are not filled with drink; ye clothe you, but there is none warm; and he that earneth wages earneth wages *to put it* into a bag with holes.

- Haggai 1:6.

2.   Purposeless life

There are those whose lifestyles reflect no genuine ambition or desire to excel.   They simply exist and "float" around through life.   They are happy to have someone labour for their joy but will not make any effort to see their dreams come true.   They want to be housed, fed, clothed and highly pampered. Many times such people do not even bathe or attend to their hair, much less clean their teeth. They have the opportunity to do so but the powers of darkness have blinded their understanding.   Their hearts have been deceived. They are slothful. Slothfulness is by far   much   worse   than   ordinary   laziness because it is laziness of the heart. They are sluggards![5]

Enoch lived for a very short time on the planet compared to most people of his time yet he left a mark behind.[6] Methuselah lived longer than anyone else. His record remains unbroken.[7] Yet as far as the scriptures tell us, he left no legacy to justify his long lifespan. Lazy people abort the calling of God upon their lives. The scriptures declare:

> 26. As vinegar to the teeth, and as smoke to the eyes, so is the sluggard to them that send him.
>
> - Proverbs 20:26.

Such people may not easily see their need for deliverance. They play the ostrich pretending curses and demons do not exist. It may be

---

[5] Proverbs 6:6-11.
[6] Genesis 5:21-24.
[7] Genesis 5:25-27.

worse if they end up in a church where God's Word is taught by ministers who lack His anointing.

The teaching ministry is of great importance to the body of Christ. However, such people need more than a beautiful theological sermon on *"Seven steps to your financial breakthrough"*.

In addition to all our wonderful teachings and great Bible expositions, such people (like every one of us) need an encounter with God! No wonder it has never been God's will for anyone to proclaim the good news without the power of the Holy Ghost![8]

3.   Perpetual health problems

> 27.   The LORD will smite thee with the botch of Egypt, and with the emerods, and with the scab, and

---

[8] Luke 24:49; Acts 1:8.

with the itch, whereof thou canst not be healed.

- Deuteronomy 28:27.

60. Moreover he will bring upon thee all the diseases of Egypt, which thou wast afraid of; and they shall cleave unto thee.

61. Also every sickness, and every plague, which *is* not written in the book of this law, them will the LORD bring upon thee, until thou be destroyed.

- Deuteronomy 28:60-61.

Many sicknesses and diseases have medical solutions. However, there are those diseases which do not seem to have any solution known to humanity. Some sicknesses and diseases defy every medical and surgical effort known to humanity. Behind them lies malicious evil spirits always working against the joy of their victims.

> 38. And he arose out of the synagogue, and entered into Simon's house. And Simon's wife's mother was taken with a great fever; and they besought him for her.

> 39. And he stood over her, and rebuked the fever; and it left her: and immediately she arose and ministered unto them.

> - Luke 4:38-39.

The Lord Jesus rebuked the fever in the life of Peter's mother in law. You cannot rebuke a thing incapable of hearing you. You rebuke someone who hears! That fever had an ability to hear and to leave. It was intelligent. There was more to the problem than the physical pain she felt.

Some sicknesses and diseases keep a program. Some people fall sick every time they have an appointment for a job. Some students always get medical or surgical problems during their examination seasons. Sicknesses and diseases always come in between them and their moments of victory. Such challenges may come along with depression, self-pity, anguish, sorrow, et cetera.

These are real spiritual problems. They should be rebuked in the Name of Jesus Christ under the anointing of the Holy Spirit. Sometimes this too will not work until some sins have been confessed and forsaken, covenants broken, et cetera.

Some diseases are in a bloodline. You cannot get cancer, asthma, or sugar diabetes from your neighbour or those you went to the same school with. You can inherit such diseases from your ancestors. They could have been in the bloodline for more than ten generations. Perhaps one person invited that problem into the family by an act of rebellion against the counsel of God!

I remember seeing a woman on Pastor Benny Hinn's "This is your day" television program. She was healed of cancer. A spirit of cancer had entered into her life when she watched a television program by psychics. Beloved, every satanic program has the potential to devastate your life by introducing a demon or more into your life. satanic programs and activities open one's life to the discretion of demonic spirits. The result is infirmity and destruction. There is more to chronic sicknesses and diseases than meets the eye!

Also where a problem keeps a program as is the case is for epilepsy, one needs more than a physical solution to the challenge. It calls for deliverance in the Name of Jesus Christ the Son of the Living God!

4.   Male and female problems

a).   Male problems:

These may include seasonal and sometimes permanent impotence, chronic venereal diseases whose origin can hardly be identified, demonic wet dreams and so much more.   There are those who in their sleep *"fornicate"* with a woman only to wake up later on and realize that woman was in the spirit realm.   That woman is what is called a *"spirit wife"; succubus.*

A spirit wife wages war against any woman in whom you express interest. It may cause you to reject women or cause women to reject you.

It may cause their premature deaths!   It regards them co-wives.   It may fight the consummation of a marriage!   It strives to influence your attitude concerning women.   It can give you a stench stronger than any perfume so that no woman stands your presence.

One does not have to be interested in a spirit wife in order to be under its bondage. It takes advantage of a person either because of a covenant he inherited or was initiated into, or because of promiscuity and licentiousness. Such a person needs to be born again and delivered by the power of God in Jesus Name (Please get my book; **"Spiritual Male Problems"**).

b). Female problems:

These may include barrenness, miscarriages, strange tormenting pains during menstruation periods, tumours and strange growths in the cervix, uterus, fallopian tubes, ovaries, or abdomen. This curse affects the area of reproduction.

Idolatry and witchcraft or any demonic arts can also lead to miscarriages and barrenness.

We read in the scriptures about idolatrous Ephraim:

11.   *As for* Ephraim, their glory shall fly away like a bird, from the birth, and from the womb, and from the conception.

12.   Though they bring up their children, yet will I bereave them, *that   there   shall* not *be* a man *left*: yea, woe also to them when I depart from them!

13.   Ephraim, as I saw Tyrus, *is* planted in a pleasant place: but Ephraim shall bring forth his children to the murderer.

14.   Give them, O LORD: what wilt thou give? give them a miscarrying womb and dry breasts.

- Hosea 9:11-14.

There are cases where a bride fails to have her marriage consummated because a demon *(spirit husband; incubus)* has blocked her. A spirit husband takes advantage of a woman during her sleep. I have ministered to some women who experienced this in broad day light. A woman does not have to consent to the act. The spirit husband assumes a sense of ownership over its victims the same way a spirit wife does to a man.

I have met cases where four generations of very beautiful women who were very highly educated, very well behaved and very wealthy as far as material possessions were concerned lived in one house. None of them had ever been to the altar with a man, before a priest! They have children with some absentee fathers but not a church wedding. Why? A spirit husband said NO to their marriages!

Some women with spirit husbands also have spirit children. They nurse children during their sleep. They may also experience invisible (and on some very rare occasions visible) children sucking their breasts. It may be hard for them to bear real children because as far as the spirit world is concerned, they are mothers!

Sometimes a spirit husband gives its victim a stench that no man is able to stand her presence. Sometimes it causes you to wet your bed so that sharing a bed with your husband is not a dream come true for both of you but a living nightmare!

The Bible is not silent about spirit beings having sexual relationships with humanity and even having *"children"* born out of those ungodly relationships:

> 1. And it came to pass, when men began to multiply on the face of the earth, and daughters were born unto them,

2.   That the sons of God saw
the   daughters   of   men   that
they *were* fair; and they took them
wives of all which they chose.

3.   And the LORD said, My spirit
shall not always strive with man,
for that he also *is* flesh: yet his
days shall be an hundred and
twenty years.

4.   There were giants in the
earth in those days; and also after
that, when the sons of God came
in unto the daughters of men, and
they bare *children* to them, the
same *became* mighty   men
which *were* of old, men of renown.

5.   And GOD saw that the
wickedness of man *was* great in
the   earth,   and *that* every
imagination of the thoughts of his
heart *was* only evil continually.

6. And it repented the LORD that he had made man on the earth, and it grieved him at his heart.

- Genesis 6:1-6.

A spirit husband cleaves to someone, a family or a bloodline because of an evil oath or covenant. The sin issue has to be dealt with. The evil covenants should be broken and then deliverance ministered in Jesus' Name!

Women who are tormented by female problems also need deliverance from spirits of grief, sadness, depression, self-pity, et cetera. I encourage you to get my book; *"Spiritual Female Problems".*

5. Perpetual marital problems

The powers of darkness detest godly homes where victorious, God-fearing children are raised. In such a home, there would be righteousness, peace and joy in the Holy Ghost.[9] The joy of the Lord is our strength.[10]

---

[9] Romans 14:17.

Not all marital challenges serve as indicators of a curse. Nevertheless, there is need to examine cases where a malicious invisible hand seems to be actively operational.

There is more to some marital challenges than what meets the eye. In cases where there is witchcraft or opposition from a spirit spouse you are likely to see unnecessary constant arguing, fighting, calling each other names. The home becomes a battleground where cursing and swearing are the trend of the day.

However, there is nothing more dangerous to a family unit or bloodline as when the Lord sets Himself against it. This normally results from much wickedness on part of the family:

> 33.   The curse of the LORD *is* in the house of the wicked: but he blesseth the habitation of the just.

---

[10] Nehemiah 8:10.

34. Surely he scorneth the scorners: but he giveth grace unto the lowly.

35. The wise shall inherit glory: but shame shall be the promotion of fools.

- Proverbs 3:33-35.

3. But fornication, and all uncleanness, or covetousness, let it not be once named among you, as becometh saints;

4. Neither filthiness, nor foolish talking, nor jesting, which are not convenient: but rather giving of thanks.

5. For this ye know, that no whoremonger, nor unclean person, nor covetous man, who is an

idolater, hath any inheritance in the kingdom of Christ and of God.

6.   Let no man deceive you with vain words: for because of these things cometh the wrath of God upon the children of disobedience.

7.   Be not ye therefore partakers with them.

- Ephesians 5:3-7.

I have known some homes where God is regarded an outlaw.   Such homes serve as workshops of the devil where works of the flesh flourish and are constantly manifested.[11] Children become unruly.   The parents fail to be good role models.   They do not have the moral authority to rebuke sin. Ungodly media, society and public schools become the counsellors of these helpless, undisciplined

---

[11] Galatians 5:19-21.

children. What a shame! Such homes easily become targets of the wrath of God.

Some families may suffer lack or end up tormented by incurable diseases just because they have chosen to be wicked! They have rejected God!

Some bloodlines have a history of separations, divorces, or chronic brutality between mates. It is a sign of a curse. It calls for deliverance from marriage breaking spirits. Chronic marital problems which seems to be inherited from one generation to another are not a blessing. They are an indicator of a curse working against a family.

6. Emotional and mental problems

These include lunacy, madness, insanity, confusion, mental breakdowns, nervous breakdowns, dissociative identity disorder, schizophrenia, brain diseases, et cetera.

Some mental illnesses and diseases can neither be treated with our modern drugs, technology, nor secular education. Psychiatrics stand helpless in face of lunacy, schizophrenia and many other mental illnesses.

Dissociative identity disorder manifests as multiple personalities in one body. It is as though you have different persons living in one body. Just like schizophrenia, its symptoms may include anxiety, anger, violence, argumentativeness, emotional distance, self-importance, delusional thoughts, hallucinations, and suicidal behavior. It leads to great mental instability.

It takes the anointing of the Holy Spirit to solve these demonic problems. Sometimes they are a result of rejection, witchcraft, rebellion, traumatic experiences, or evil covenants.

28. The LORD shall smite thee with madness, and blindness, and astonishment of heart:

29. And thou shalt grope at noonday, as the blind gropeth in darkness, and thou shalt not prosper in thy ways: and thou shalt be only oppressed and spoiled evermore, and no man shall save *thee*.

- Deuteronomy 28:28-29.

Concerning mental illnesses, the deliverance minister should be anointed, loving and patient.

Mental diseases may include tumours and strange growths in or near the brain. In some cases where the inevitable risky surgery has been successful, you may find the problem happening again and again finally affecting the spiritual, mental, emotional and physical stability of the person. Brain diseases can be as many as their victims are!

We are so grateful to God for the medical experts of our times. Life on earth would be so miserable without them. The Lord Jesus was happy with a Samaritan who treated someone's wounds and paid his hospital bill.[12] Hospitals are a blessing! However, the medical world is yet to discover a drug, which saves lost souls and casts demons out! The church of Jesus Christ knows it takes more than drugs and academic theories to address these challenges. It takes the incorruptible Word of the Living God. Our Lord Jesus chirst in His fullness is the answer. The painful truth is that some builders keep on rejecting this Chief Corner Stone.[13]

1.   And they came over unto the other side of the sea, into the country of the Gadarenes.

---

[12] Luke 10:30-37.
[13] Matthew 12:10; Mark 12:10; Luke 20:17; Acts 4:11; 26:26; Ephesians 2:20; 1 Peter 2:6–7.

2.   And when he was come out of the ship, immediately there met him out of the tombs a man with an unclean spirit,

3.   Who had *his* dwelling among the tombs; and no man could bind him, no, not with chains:

4.   Because that he had been often bound with fetters and chains, and the chains had been plucked asunder by him, and the fetters broken in pieces: neither could any *man* tame him.

5.   And always, night and day, he was in the mountains, and in the tombs, crying, and cutting himself with stones.

6.   But when he saw Jesus afar off, he ran and worshipped him,

7.   And cried with a loud voice, and said, What have I to do with thee, Jesus, *thou* Son of the most high God? I adjure thee by God, that thou torment me not.

8.   For he said unto him, Come out of the man, *thou* unclean spirit.

9.   And   he   asked   him, What *is* thy   name?   And   he answered,   saying,   My name *is* Legion: for we are many.

10.   And he besought him much that he would not send them away out of the country.

11.   Now there was there nigh unto the mountains a great herd of swine feeding.

12.   And all the devils besought him, saying, Send us into the

swine, that we may enter into them.

13. And forthwith Jesus gave them leave. And the unclean spirits went out, and entered into the swine: and the herd ran violently down a steep place into the sea, (they were about two thousand;) and were choked in the sea.

14. And they that fed the swine fled, and told *it* in the city, and in the country. And they went out to see what it was that was done.

15. And they come to Jesus, and see him that was possessed with the devil, and had the legion, sitting, and clothed, and in his right mind: and they were afraid.

- Mark 5:1-15.

7. Recurring premature deaths in the family

Righteousness, the fear of God and obedience to His council can prolong our lives. For example, the Word of God tells us:

> 12. Honour thy father and thy mother: that thy days may be long upon the land which the LORD thy God giveth thee.
>
> - Exodus 20:12.

> 7. And Er, Judah's firstborn, was wicked in the sight of the LORD; and the LORD slew him.

> 8. And Judah said unto Onan, Go in unto thy brother's wife, and marry her, and raise up seed to thy brother.

9.   And Onan knew that the seed should not be his; and it came to pass, when he went in unto his brother's wife, that he spilled *it* on the ground, lest that he should give seed to his brother.

10.   And the thing which he did displeased the LORD: wherefore he slew him also.

- Genesis 38:7-10.

Death is an enemy.[14] It is true that every human being has an appointment with physical death.[15] However, it is equally true that God never intended us to have a short lifespan.[16] God's love and concern for the widows and orphans[17] are part of the evidence that He did not plan for people to die young leaving behind generations of suffering,

---

[14] 1 Corinthians 15:26.
[15] Hebrews 9:27.
[16] Genesis 6:3; Psalm 91:16.
[17] Exodus 22:22.

helpless orphans, or traumatized parents and loved ones.

The curse of recurring premature deaths in the family has its roots in wickedness on part of the affected and at times strengthened by evil covenants or oaths made to powers of darkness. I prayed for a young man in whose family all the males would die at twenty-nine years of age. How did this start? His father (now dead) had sacrificed his firstborn son after his twenty-ninth birthday at an altar in a witchdoctor's shrine.

The blood of his son became the blood of the evil covenant entered into with the bloodthirsty powers of darkness. The powers of darkness were now welcome to be members of his family and the lives of all his descendants were at their disposal for protection in case the family honoured the covenant and *"chastisement"* in case this covenant was violated. Little did he know that the chastisement promised was an ambiguous word which included death and destruction. In exchange, he was granted wealth, fame and many wives.

After some years, this man and his family began to observe an evil trend. They had the wealth, the fame and they were greatly admired by many people but they missed out on peace, joy and an assurance for safety. Their "palace" was such a demonic centre where violence, sexual sins, and witchcraft reigned. The men in the family would all die at twenty-nine years. Some of them died because of car accidents, water, electricity or fire. Some of them would go to sleep healthy only to die mysteriously in their sleep. Others would contract diseases to which the medical world did not seem to have any answers. Suicides too were a common occurrence in the family.

This young man repented, confessed his father's iniquities, renounced the oaths and pledges made to the evil spirits, then those evil covenants where broken and he enjoyed the reality of true deliverance in Jesus' Name.

There are families where people die young. In some families those who are poor and miserable live long but if one gets some money so that he or she begins to be the joy of the family, then death strikes causing deep sorrow to the hearts of the family.

The father of one young man committed suicide using his necktie while in the bathroom. This young man, my former schoolmate ended his life the same way. I have ministered deliverance to people who were on the verge of suicide. Many of them come from bloodlines where suicides were the trend of the day.

Deliverance from spirits of suicide needs more than what a good psychologist or psychiatrist can give. It is not unheard of for some of these intellectual giants to take their lives too. It takes more than the arm of the flesh. One needs the anointing of the Holy Ghost to break these yokes of bondage!

27.   Depart from evil, and do good; and dwell for evermore.

28. For the LORD loveth judgment, and forsaketh not his saints; they are preserved for ever: but the seed of the wicked shall be cut off.

- Psalm 37:27-28.

22. But the wicked shall be cut off from the earth, and the transgressors shall be rooted out of it.

- Proverbs 2:22.

17. Be not over much wicked, neither be thou foolish: why shouldest thou die before thy time?

- Ecclesiastes 7:17.

8. Inclination to accidents

There are no accidents in the spirit realm. When some ugly thing happens abruptly, in the physical realm we call that "ACCIDENTAL". It has taken us by surprise but God knew it, He permitted it.

29.   Are not two sparrows sold for a farthing? and one of them shall not fall on the ground without your Father.

- Matthew 10:29.

Why does God permit accidents?   Some people *'seem'* to have answers to every question.   They are so *'knowledgeable'* they could attempt to explain anything in the universe.   Yet the more they talk the more ignorant they sound!

29.   The   secret *things*   *belong* unto   the   LORD   our   God: but those *things*   *which*   *are* revealed *belong* unto us and to our children for   ever,   that *we* may   do   all   the words of this law.

- Deuteronomy 29:29.

Not   everyone   who   gets   involved   in   an accident   is   a   victim   of   a   curse.   However,

165

there are people in life who are prone to accidents all the time. These accidents may be big or small. They may be due to the technology of our day; electric shocks, plane crashes, car accidents, et cetera. Some people are ever choking on food. Others are ever accidentally cutting their fingers or some other parts of their body. Some experience burns and scolds or always knock their foot on a stone, breaking or spraining their ankles. Perhaps those accidents concern your wealth. They come against you and against your investments (farms, buildings, automobiles, et cetera) with such urgency, frequency and malice that you are tempted to feel demoralized and disillusioned.

13.   And there was a day when his sons and his daughters *were* eating and drinking wine in their eldest brother's house:

14.   And there came a messenger unto Job, and said, The

oxen were plowing, and the asses feeding beside them:

15.   And the Sabeans fell *upon them*, and took them away; yea, they have slain the servants with the edge of the sword; and I only am escaped alone to tell thee.

16.   While he *was* yet speaking, there came also another, and said, The fire of God is fallen from heaven, and hath burned up the sheep, and the servants, and consumed them; and I only am escaped alone to tell thee.

17.   While he *was* yet speaking, there came also another, and said, The Chaldeans made out three bands, and fell upon the camels, and have carried them away, yea, and slain the servants with the

edge of the sword; and I only am escaped alone to tell thee.

18.   While he *was* yet speaking, there came also another, and said, Thy sons and thy daughters *were* eating and drinking wine in their eldest brother's house:

19.   And, behold, there came a great wind from the wilderness, and smote the four corners of the house, and it fell upon the young men, and they are dead; and I only am escaped alone to tell thee.

- Job 1:13-19.

None of the evil things listed took God by surprise. He permitted them. Job and his friends were taken unawares.

There is always a tendency for some people to blame God for everything when tragedies strike[18] and either curse[19] Him to His face or resort to self- pity, grief, and depression.[20] Others try to find some escape route through intoxicants.[21] Intoxicants do not break curses. On the contrary, they actually facilitate their offensive against you. They are the worst friends you can ever run to in times of trouble. God alone is the answer.[22] The only way to God is through His Son Jesus Christ.[23]

Job tried to justify himself.[24] That does not work! satan had outwitted him by destroying the animals. Job had no blood sacrifice, therefore his sins remained uncovered! Perhaps things would have been different if he had repented for his lack of faith in God's protection,[25] for the sins of his ungodly children[26] ungodly nagging wife,[27] et cetera.

---

[18] Job 1:20-21; 2:10.
[19] Job 2:9.
[20] Job 3:11; 24–26.
[21] Proverbs 31:6-7.
[22] Proverbs 18:10; Nahum 1:7.
[23] John 14:6; Acts 4:12
[24] Job 6:28-30.
[25] Job 3:24-26.
[26] Job 1:4-5.
[27] Job 2:9-10; 19:17,

It is interesting to note that Job's victory did not come about until after his shedding of some animal blood[28] and unselfish prayer.[29] We do not need to shed any blood any longer. We apply the blood of Jesus Christ the Son of the living God![30]

The solution lies in identifying our enemy and fighting those diabolic spiritual forces by the revealed counsel of God.[31] This kind of curse normally has close links with premature deaths in the family.

9. Abuse and lack of favour

The ninth indicator of a curse is a life marked by abuse and mistreatment. Victims of this curse become candidates of no favour, no mercy and no grace! This may include receiving verbal threats and insults for a

---

[28] Job 42:7-9.
[29] Job 42:10.
[30] 1 John 1:7.
[31] 2 Corinthians 10:3-6; Ephesians 6:10-18.

reason that causes other people to be praised.

A person struggling with this curse may do something good but the praise goes to other people all the time. He may have access to wealth but can never enjoy it. He or she is only oppressed and robbed all the time.

> 30. Thou shalt betroth a wife, and another man shall lie with her: thou shalt build an house, and thou shalt not dwell therein: thou shalt plant a vineyard, and shalt not gather the grapes thereof.

> 31. Thine ox *shall be* slain before thine eyes, and thou shalt not eat thereof: thine ass *shall be* violently taken away from before thy face, and shall not be restored to thee: thy sheep *shall be* given unto thine enemies, and

thou shalt have none to rescue *them*.

32. Thy sons and thy daughters *shall be* given unto another people, and thine eyes shall look, and fail *with longing* for them all the day long: and *there shall be* no might in thine hand.

33. The fruit of thy land, and all thy labours, shall a nation which thou knowest not eat up; and thou shalt be only oppressed and crushed alway:

34. So that thou shalt be mad for the sight of thine eyes which thou shalt see.

- Deuteronomy 28:30-34.

-

This curse denies you the right to enjoy your children or the fruits of your labour. You only labour for the benefit of other nations and people.

There are those who are victims of physical abuse all the time. They always bear wounds of someone's wrath even when the fight or quarrel does not concern them or just because they became arbitrators! Sometimes robbers, lunatics, drug addicts, or even some seemingly good people who happen to detest their company assault them.

Cain expected to be injured by everyone he would meet after a curse had come upon his life. He said, *"and it shall come to pass, that every one that findeth me shall slay me"* (Genesis 4:14).

Abusive relationships, rejection, molestation, rape, incest all fall under this category.

A number of people have suffered emotional and spiritual abuse. I remember praying for a young woman, an ex-prostitute who said there were times in her life when demonic spirits would rape her. Day or night, time did not matter. They always took advantage of her at their discretion, against her will! There are some men as well whom demonic spirits have abused sexually. Some demons strangle their victims and torment them in such a way that those people end up living lonely, fearful lives.

This curse demoralizes a person; kills one's self-esteem and eventually destroys the whole person negatively affecting all those who are under that person's authority. It can affect an individual, a family, a community, or even nations.

10. Living life as a fugitive or vagabond

After Cain murdered his brother, he was cursed. The curse was to the effect that he would be a fugitive and a vagabond:

11.　And　now *art* thou　cursed from the earth, which hath opened her mouth to receive thy brother's blood from thy hand;

12.　When thou tillest the ground, it shall not henceforth yield unto thee her strength; a fugitive and a vagabond shalt thou be in the earth.

13.　And Cain said unto the LORD, My punishment *is* greater than I can bear.

14.　Behold, thou hast driven me out this day from the face of the earth; and from thy face shall I be hid; and I shall be a fugitive and a vagabond in the earth; and it shall come to pass, *that* every one that findeth me shall slay me.

- Genesis 4:11-14.

A vagabond is a homeless wonderer. There are people who move from place to place without any fixed residence. Others cannot keep a job.

Others keep on moving from one relationship to another without ever settling down to establish a home. Others move from one church to another, to another, to another, all the time. Of course, it is all right for any saint to depart from an ungodly, cultic congregation.[32] The painful surprise of it all is that some of the churches where a vagabond may not have settled are very good Bible believing, Bible practicing congregations.

A vagabond lives a life of poverty not only because he or she never settles down to concentrate on any income generating project that demands their patience, commitment and sacrifice, but also because they need a spiritual breakthrough.

---

[32] 2 Corinthians 6:14-18.

A fugitive lives their lives as though they are fleeing from prosecution or persecution. Just like vagabonds, they too cannot live in one place, much less trust anyone.

Just like Cain some people are vagabonds and live their lives as fugitives simply because they or their ancestors are guilty of some innocent human blood.

11. Groping like the blind

28. The LORD shall smite thee with madness, and blindness, and astonishment of heart:

29. And thou shalt grope at noonday, as the blind gropeth in darkness, and thou shalt not prosper in thy ways: and thou shalt be only oppressed and spoiled

evermore, and no man shall save *thee*.

- Deuteronomy 29:28-29.

The kind of life indicated here is so full of hindrances and frustrations. No matter what somebody does, they can never be victorious. Life to such a person seems excursions in the dark! They do not have a sense of direction. They encounter great hindrances, no matter what they do. They are oppressed and robbed all the time yet no one seems to come to their rescue as these invisible capricious forces kill, steal, and destroy their lives.[33]

23. And thy heaven that *is* over thy head shall be brass, and the earth that is under thee*shall be* iron.

- Deuteronomy 28:23.

---

[33] John 10:10.

They do not seem to have any favour from heaven. The earth behaves so unfriendly towards them. They "grope at noonday, as the blind gropeth in darkness"- Deuteronomy 28:29.

12. Nightmares, sleepless nights and a life hanging in doubt

66. And thy life shall hang in doubt before thee; and thou shalt fear day and night, and shalt have none assurance of thy life:

67. In the morning thou shalt say, Would God it were even! and at even thou shalt say, Would God it were morning! for the fear of thine heart wherewith thou shalt fear, and for the sight of thine eyes which thou shalt see.

- Deutronomy 28:66-67.

Nights seem unnecessarily long and endless when characterized with sleeplessness or horrifying dreams. Some people have to sleep with lights on every night for fear of demonic spirits strangling them or abusing them sexually. Others fear to fall asleep lest they get a nightmare.

Nightmares and hallucinations are not the result of having worked so hard during the day and then winding the day off with a good heavy meal before one falls asleep. These are real spiritual problems whose origin is hell. They instil fear in the life of the victim; the fear of darkness, the fear of falling asleep. Fear hath torment.[34] Fear serves as an invitation for evil to come your way.[35] It is faith in the devil's ability to destroy you. Fear opens the door of your life to evil spirits to destroy you.

Job narrates his ordeal with nightmares. Anyone who reads through the first two chapters of the book of Job notices how satan

---

[34] 1 John 4:18.
[35] Job 3:24–26; Proverbs 10:24.

launched a vicious attack against Job, his family and property. It is evident this was the work of satan and his cohorts against him

13.   When I say, My bed shall comfort me, my couch shall ease my complaint;

14.   Then thou scarest me with dreams, and terrifiest me through visions:

15.   So that my soul chooseth strangling, *and* death rather than my life.

16.   I loathe *it*; I would not live alway: let me alone; for my days *are* vanity.

- Job 7:13-16.

There are those who cannot fall asleep without the use of drugs or intoxicants. That is not God plan for our lives. Sweet sound sleep is the blessing of God.

> 2. *It is* vain for you to rise up early, to sit up late, to eat the bread of sorrows: *for* so he giveth his beloved sleep.
>
> - Psalm 127:2.

Beloved in Christ, your body is the temple of God.[36] You need to take good care of it so you can serve God for a longer time here on earth. Your body needs hygiene, good care, exercise, good feeding, and adequate rest. The Word of God warns us about laziness. However, rising up early should not be unprofitable. Some people rise up so early every day, not to pray, study their Bible, or do anything profitable but just to sit upon their beds and WORRY!

---

[36] 1 Corinthians 3:16-17; 6:19; 2 Corinthians 6:16.

Others are afraid of daytime. Dawn reminds them about their daily challenges. Daytime seems long and endless. Sometimes their days are full of traumatic experiences. Some people feel haunted all the time. They are worried about the past. They fear the present. They dread the future! They are more conscious about what satan can do against them than what God desires to do for them.

> 24. For my sighing cometh before I eat, and my roarings are poured out like the waters.

> 25. For the thing which I greatly feared is come upon me, and that which I was afraid of is come unto me.

> 26. I was not in safety, neither had I rest, neither was I quiet; yet trouble came.

> - Job 3:24-26.

Nightmares, sleepless nights and a life hanging in doubt are not a blessing. *"For so He giveth His beloved sleep"* - Psalm 127:2c.

Chapter 9.

How to obtain deliverance

The greatest hindrance to obtaining deliverance is sin. Sin makes you a slave to satan and so denies you access to the presence of God.

God is not interested in listening to the wicked. Sin concealed or revealed, is still an abomination to his sight!

> 18. If I regard iniquity in my heart, the Lord will not hear *me*:
> - Psalm 66:18.

1.   Behold, the LORD's hand is
not shortened, that it cannot save;
neither his ear heavy, that it cannot
hear:

2.   But your iniquities have
separated between you and your
God, and your sins have hid
His face from you, that he will not
hear.

3.   For your hands are defiled
with blood, and your fingers with
iniquity; your lips have spoken lies,
your tongue hath muttered
perverseness.

4.   None calleth for justice,
nor *any* pleadeth for truth: they
trust in vanity, and speak lies; they
conceive mischief, and bring forth
iniquity.

- Isaiah 59:1-4.

31. Now we know that God heareth not sinners: but if any man be a worshipper of God, and doeth his will, him He heareth.

- John 9:31.

There are four steps to obtaining true deliverance:

i.   Repentance;

ii.   Renouncing and breaking all ungodly covenants and ties;

iii.   Declaring who we are in Christ, What He is in us and what belongs to us in Him;

iv.   Rebuking of evil spirits in the Name of Jesus.

i.   Repentance

Beloved, the enemy of your soul, satan hates your repentance because it removes his legal ground of accusation against you.

Repentance demands more than a confession of your sins to God. There is need for you to forsake your sins and turn completely back to God.

> 13.   He that covereth his sins shall not prosper: but whoso confesseth and forsaketh *them* shall have mercy.
>
> - Proverbs 28:13.

A story is told of a man who stole some money from his place of work. When he went back to his house he knelt down to pray and he confessed his sins; *"Father, I am sorry for the one hundred dollar bill which I stole from my place of work. Please forgive me in the Name of Jesus. Amen. Father I would also like to repent in advance concerning the other one hundred dollar bill that I left behind. I feel I cannot resist the temptation to steal it as well. I am going back to the office to collect it!"* That is what many of us have done in our Christian walk. We have confessed our sins but have not forsaken them. That is not true repentance because there is no forsaking of sins. Some people confess adultery or addiction to intoxicants all the time and yet continue to live their lives as slaves to those sins.

Others prefer giving big sacrifices and gifts to God instead of repenting, obeying Him and living disciplined holy lives. There is a difference between working hard and doing the will of God.[1] Obedience is better than sacrifice.[2]

> 14. If my people, which are called by My Name, shall humble

---

[1] Matthew 7:21–23.
[2] 1 Samuel 15:22.

themselves, and pray, and seek My face, and turn from their wicked ways; then will I hear from heaven, and will forgive their sin, and will heal their land.

- 2 Chronicles 7:14.

2 Chronicles 7:14 is a very amazing verse in the Word of God. They are God's people. They are called (named after Him and referred to) by His Name. Yet they are not humble. They hardly pray. If they ever pray, it is never to seek His face. They have not turned from their wicked ways! Therefore, God does not hear them. He has not forgiven their sin. Their land cannot be healed in such a state!

There is need for God's people to humble themselves before Him. There is need for God's people to pray without ceasing, with all prayer and supplication in the spirit. There is need for us to seek His face. Prayer should not be just about asking God for things. We should come before Him because He is,[3] not because He has! As we pray there is need for us not only to confess our sins but also to utterly forsake our sinful, wicked ways.[4] We should abstain from all appearance of evil. Then we will enjoy the fellowship of the Father, Son,[5] and Holy Spirit.[6] The sense of guilt and unworthiness will disappear from our hearts because the blood of Jesus Christ will have cleansed us from all unrighteousness.[7] Then we will be healed, strengthened, and revived. We will enjoy the blessing of God every day. Repentance. Repent. Repent!

When we repent, we do not only deal with our sins as individuals. We should also confess and forsake our corporate sins as families, bloodlines, churches, companies, nations, et cetera. The book of Nehemiah exemplifies this.

---

[3] Hebrews 11:6.
[4] Proverb 28:13.
[5] 1 John 1:3.
[6] 2 Corinthians 13:14.
[7] 1 John 1:7-9.

1.   Now in the twenty and fourth day of this month the children of Israel were assembled with fasting, and with sackclothes, and earth upon them.

2.   And the seed of Israel separated themselves from all strangers, and stood and confessed their sins, and the iniquities of their fathers.

3.   And they stood up in their place, and read in the book of the law of the LORD their God *one* fourth part of the day; and *another* fourth part they confessed, and worshipped the LORD their God.

- Nehemiah 9:1-3.

Nehemiah 9:3 reveals some great truths. Not only did they confess and forsake their sins as individuals, families and bloodlines, they also read in the book of the law, and confessed (acknowledged, declared) and worshipped the LORD their God. True repentance calls us back to God and His Word! So we may worship Him in spirit and in truth. Repent!

In cases where possible, repentance should be accompanied with acts of restitution. We read in Luke:

> 8. And Zacchaeus stood, and said unto the Lord; Behold, Lord, the half of my goods I give to the poor; and if I have taken any thing from any man by false accusation, I restore *him* fourfold.

> 9. And Jesus said unto him, This day is salvation come to this house, for so much as he also is a son of Abraham.

> -   Luke 19:8-9.

As soon as Zacchaeus purposed to restore what he had stolen, the Lord Jesus, declared salvation to his house! Repent! Repent! Repent!

ii.   Renouncing and breaking all ungodly covenants and ties

In addition to our repentance, there is need for us to renounce and break all our ungodly covenants, commitments, ties, oaths, and pledges. Satan is legalistic! Some evil spirits cling to certain individuals, families, bloodlines, societies, nations, et cetera, just because those people have never renounced and broken the covenants by which satan and his cohorts were invited and honoured!

Some demonic problems have oppressed certain bloodlines for centuries just because their ancestors made oaths and pledges to the powers of darkness.

Words! Words! Words are so important. Bondage comes by words.[8] Salvation comes by words.[9] Condemnation comes by words![10]

---

[8] Proverbs 6:2.
[9] Romans 10:9-10.

Justification comes by words![11] That is what our Lord Jesus said!

We read about the breaking of ungodly marriage ties in the book of Ezra.[12] In our dispensation, this cannot be an excuse for divorce by people whose marriages have been blessed by the church. The children of Israel knew that it was an act of rebellion for them to be involved in sexual relationships and marriages with the gentiles. Such relationships would open Israel up to the iniquities of those gentile nations.

I know this is a sensitive, controversial issue but depending on our level of maturity in the things of God, there would be wisdom in praying and working towards a marriage that will win the smile of Jesus! That is my counsel to the unmarried. To those who are married, please stick to Hebrews 13:4.

---

[10] Matthew 12:37.
[11] Matthew 12:37.
[12] Ezra 9-10.

4.   Marriage *is* honourable in all, and the bed undefiled: but whoremongers and adulterers God will judge.

- Hebrews 13:4.

9.   And I say unto you, Whosoever shall put away his wife, except *it be* for fornication, and shall marry another, committeth adultery: and whoso marrieth her which is put away doth commit adultery.

-    Matthew 19:9.

We need to renounce and break all our ungodly ties whether they be physical ties, soul ties or spiritual ties.   We need to dissociate ourselves from every form of evil bondage.   We should abstain from all appearance of evil.[13]

---

[13] 1 Thessalonians 5:22.

iii. Declaring who we are in Christ, What He is in us and what belongs to us in Him.

Our declaration of who we are in Christ is so important. We need to know who we are because of the redemptive work of Christ. We need to declare it all the time. There are verses in the Bible, especially in the epistles, that tell us who we are in Him because of His finished work at Calvary and what fully belongs to us in Him. These verses contain phrases such as *"in Him"*, *"in whom"*, *"through Christ"* and *"through Him"*. For example:

> 28. For in him we live, and move, and have our being; as certain also of your own poets have said, For we are also His offspring.
>
> - Acts 17:28.

> 37. Nay, in all these things we are more than conquerors through Him that loved us.
>
> - Romans 8:37.

17.   Therefore if any man *be* in Christ, *he is* a new creature: old things are passed away; behold, all things are become new.

- 2 Corinthians 5:17.

7.   In Whom we have redemption through His blood, the forgiveness of sins, according to the riches of His grace;

- Ephesians 1:7.

13.   I can do all things through Christ which strengtheneth me.

- Philippians 4:13.

In addition to knowing who we are in Him and what we have because of His redemptive work, we should also learn to make our boast in Him.[14] We should never suffocate Him Who lives in us. Our testimony of Who He is and what He can do in and through us is such

---

[14] Psalm 44:8

a great weapon the forces of darkness can never stand.[15] It also builds our faith in Him. For example:

16. Know ye not that ye are the temple of God, and *that* the Spirit of God dwelleth in you?

- 1 Corinthians 3:16.

13. For it is God which worketh in you both to will and to do of *his* good pleasure.

- Philippians 2:13.

4. Ye are of God, little children, and have overcome them: because greater is He that is in you, than he that is in the world.

- 1 John 4:4.

---

[15] Revelation 12:11.

iv. Rebuking of evil spirits in the name of Jesus Christ

The first three steps already mentioned are very important as far as deliverance is concerned; repentance, the breaking of ungodly ties and covenants and a bold declaration of what Christ is in us, and who we are in Him because of His finished work at Calvary. However, equally important is this fourth step: the rebuking of evil spirits in Jesus Name!

In the Bible, we find a number of occasions when the Lord Jesus commanded evil spirits to come out of their captives.[16] demonic spirits can and should be addressed because they have the ability to hear, and they are subject to us in Jesus Name![17] It is our right and obligation to cast demons out in Jesus' Name.

I met a wonderful man of God who did not

---

[16] Matthew 8:16; 17:14–18; Mark 1:21–28; 5:1–13; Luke 4:38–41
[17] Mark 16:16; Luke 10:17–19; Acts 16:16–18.

believe in rebuking demons. He said all we needed to do was worship God and the anointing would take care of that. That is heresy. If Jesus Christ (the Anointed One) rebuked demons, who is or who can ever be more anointed than Christ Himself!

It is not wrong for us to command mountains to move out of our ways. We should speak to the mountains in Jesus' Name:

> 23. For verily I say unto you, That whosoever shall say unto this mountain, Be thou removed, and be thou cast into the sea; and shall not doubt in his heart, but shall believe that those things which he saith shall come to pass; he shall have whatsoever he saith.
>
> - Mark 11:23.

> 7. Submit yourselves therefore to God. Resist the devil, and he will flee from you.
>
> - James 4:7.

There are times when a person delivered from demonic bondage may need some special care, or a prayer for healing. There are occasions in the Bible when the evil spirits would throw their victims down and express so much hatred and anger against them.

We read in the gospel according to Mark:

14. And when He came to *His* disciples, He saw a great multitude about them, and the scribes questioning with them.

15. And straightway all the people, when they beheld Him, were greatly amazed, and running to *Him* saluted Him.

16. And He asked the scribes, What question ye with them?

17. And one of the multitude answered and said, Master, I have brought unto thee my son, which hath a dumb spirit;

18. And wheresoever he taketh him, he teareth him: and he foameth, and gnasheth with his teeth, and pineth away: and I spake to thy disciples that they should cast him out; and they could not.

19. He answereth him, and saith, O faithless generation, how long shall I be with you? how long shall I suffer you? bring him unto Me.

20. And they brought him unto Him: and when He saw him, straightway the spirit tare him; and he fell on the ground, and wallowed foaming.

21. And He asked his father, How long is it ago since this came unto him? And he said, Of a child.

22. And ofttimes it hath cast him into the fire, and into the waters, to destroy him: but if Thou canst do any thing, have compassion on us, and help us.

23. Jesus said unto him, If thou canst believe, all things *are* possible to him that believeth.

24. And straightway the father of the child cried out, and said with tears, Lord, I believe; help Thou mine unbelief.

25. When Jesus saw that the people came running together, He rebuked the foul spirit, saying unto him, *Thou* dumb and deaf spirit, I

charge thee, come out of him, and enter no more into him.

26.   And *the spirit* cried, and rent him sore, and came out of him: and he was as one dead; insomuch that many said, He is dead.

27.   But Jesus took him by the hand, and lifted him up; and he arose.

- Mark 9:14–27.

No wonder the Lord Jesus Lifted him up! A fresh touch from Jesus was indispensable for this young man who had fallen *"as one dead; in so much that many said, He is dead"*. The evil spirit had rent him sore before coming out of him. As occasion may demand, it is always important to pray for healing after a deliverance session.

Chapter 10.

A word

to the deliverance minister

1.   Submission to God

It is very important for the deliverance minister to be born again and to live a life pleasant to God.   Sin makes one a servant to unrighteousness.[1]   If you live a sinful life then your master is satan.[2]   You cannot exercise

---

[1] Romans 6:16.
[2] 1 John 3:8.

authority over your master.[3] Your submission to God should be complete before you can resist the devil effectively.

> 7.   Submit yourselves therefore to God. Resist the devil, and he will flee from you.
>
> - James 4:7.

Our obedience to God should be complete, lacking in nothing if the weapons of our warfare are to be used 100% effectively.[4] According to the Word of God, 99% obedience to God is rebellion.[5] We cannot call it obedience when we choose to obey God in some things and reject His counsel in other areas of our lives.

2.   Keep your eyes open

It is important to keep your eyes open while casting demons out. That way you can easily

---

[3] Matthew 10:24.
[4] 2 Corinthians 10:3–6.
[5] 1 Samuel 15:1-26.

monitor every demonic manifestation so as to be more helpful to the person you are praying for and more protective of yourself too. If not fully subdued in Jesus Name, demons can use their victim (the subject of deliverance) to assault the deliverance minister.

> 13. Then certain of the vagabond Jews, exorcists, took upon them to call over them which had evil spirits the name of the Lord Jesus, saying, We adjure you by Jesus whom Paul preacheth.

> 14. And there were seven sons of *one* Sceva, a Jew, *and* chief of the priests, which did so.

> 15. And the evil spirit answered and said, Jesus I know, and Paul I know; but who are ye?

> 16. And the man in whom the evil spirit was leaped on them, and

overcame them, and prevailed
against them, so that they fled out
of that house naked and wounded.

- Acts 19:13-16.

3.   Do not compromise with demons

The deliverance minister should not
compromise his stand just because an evil
spirit has screamed or expressed frustration. It
is not a sin to torment demons.[6]

Sometimes a demon may plead for mercy. At
times they may request not to be sent out of a
particular territory.[7] They may be territorial,
influencing the events of a region.   They
would do anything within their limited ability to
remain in charge of that territory unless a
servant of God exercises the power of God
over them in Jesus' Name.   Such was the
case in Samaria until Philip went to that city
"and preached Christ unto them".[8]

---

[6] Matthew 8:28-29
[7] Mark 5:10.
[8] Acts 8:5-13.

However, one of the greatest desires demons have is to inhabit flesh and blood. That is why our families and pets have to be covered by the blood of Jesus Christ before we start casting demons out. Covering our families and pets with the blood of Jesus is not a physical act. We do that by declaring the blood of Jesus Christ over their lives. The blood of Jesus deals such a deathblow to the activities of satan.[9]

1.   And they came over unto the other side of the sea, into the country of the Gadarenes.

2.   And when He was come out of the ship, immediately there met him out of the tombs a man with an unclean spirit,

---

[9] Revelation 12:11.

3.   Who had *his* dwelling among the tombs; and no man could bind him, no, not with chains:

4.   Because that he had been often bound with fetters and chains, and the chains had been plucked asunder by him, and the fetters broken in pieces: neither could any *man* tame him.

5.   And always, night and day, he was in the mountains, and in the tombs, crying, and cutting himself with stones.

6.   But when he saw Jesus afar off, he ran and worshipped him,

7.   And cried with a loud voice, and said, What have I to do with Thee, Jesus, *thou* Son of the most high God? I adjure thee by God, that thou torment me not.

8.   For he said unto him, Come out of the man, *thou* unclean spirit.

9.   And he asked him, What *is* thy name? And he answered, saying, My name *is* Legion: for we are many.

10.   And he besought Him much that he would not send them away out of the country.

11.   Now there was there nigh unto the mountains a great herd of swine feeding.

12.   And all the devils besought Him, saying, Send us into the swine, that we may enter into them.

13.   And forthwith Jesus gave them leave. And the unclean spirits went out, and entered into

the swine: and the herd ran violently down a steep place into the sea, (they were about two thousand;) and were choked in the sea.

-       Mark 5:1-13.

4.   Love, holiness and compassion

The deliverance ministers should do their best not to stray out of the boundaries of holiness, the God-kind of love and compassion. A full manifestation of the fruit of the spirit is required in the life of the deliverance minister because some demons may try to provoke you to anger, tempting you to think it is the person you are praying for who is insolent. The second reason is that deliverance sessions are not necessarily clean. They may, at times be filled with so much spitting, vomiting, sneezing, et cetera.

18.   And wheresoever he taketh him, he teareth him: and he

foameth, and gnasheth with his teeth, and pineth away: and I spake to Thy disciples that they should cast him out; and they could not.

19. He answereth him, and saith, O faithless generation, how long shall I be with you? how long shall I suffer you? bring him unto me.

20. And they brought him unto Him: and when he saw Him, straightway the spirit tare him; and he fell on the ground, and wallowed foaming.

- Mark 9:18-20.

5. Patience

There is always need for patience. Sometimes a deliverance session might require more time than you are prepared to spend. If such a session is conducted hurriedly so much pain and damage can be caused.

Some evil spirits have lived in certain bloodlines for centuries. They may have lived in that individual for all his or her lifetime. It is as if they are part of that individual's life. In such cases some internal organs may be damaged as these malevolent beings are forced to flee. No wonder it is always important to minister healing to some people after their deliverance.

> 25. When Jesus saw that the people came running together, He rebuked the foul spirit, saying unto him, *Thou* dumb and deaf spirit, I charge thee, come out of him, and enter no more into him.

> 26. And *the spirit* cried, and rent him sore, and came out of him: and

he was as one dead; insomuch that many said, He is dead.

27.   But Jesus took him by the hand, and lifted him up; and he arose.

-    Mark 9:25-27.

6.   Names of demons do not matter

You do not need to know the first or last name of an evil spirit before you can cast it out. You can identify an evil spirit by its works and cast it out. Some evil spirits are dumb and deaf. Others are spirits infirmity.[10] The list could go on and on. It is scripturally okay to address them by their activities.

25.   When Jesus saw that the people came running together, He

---

[10] Luke 13:11.

rebuked the foul spirit, saying unto him, *Thou* dumb and deaf spirit, I charge thee, come out of him, and enter no more into him.

26.   And *the spirit* cried, and rent him sore, and came out of him:

- Mark 9:25-26a.

7.   Casting out demons is part of the great commission

Casting demons out is not a reserve of the great apostles and prophets or archbishops. It is part of the great commission.

15.   And he said unto them, Go ye into all the world, and preach the gospel to every creature.

16. He that believeth and is baptized shall be saved; but he that believeth not shall be damned.

17. And these signs shall follow them that believe; In My Name shall they cast out devils; they shall speak with new tongues;

18. They shall take up serpents; and if they drink any deadly thing, it shall not hurt them; they shall lay hands on the sick, and they shall recover.

- Mark 16:15-18.

Ministering deliverance to those oppressed or bound by devils is the right and obligation of every true believer just like winning souls for the Kingdom of God or praying for someone's healing. The gospel also includes the blessing of speaking with new tongues and immunity against serpents and poisonous foodstuffs.

8.   Do not be puffed up

It is not the will of God for you to be puffed up just because a demon has obeyed you in Jesus' Name.   There is something greater. The greatest miracle is salvation of the soul.

> 17.   And the seventy returned again with joy, saying, Lord, even the devils are subject unto us through thy name.

> 18.   And he said unto them, I beheld Satan as lightning fall from heaven.

> 19.   Behold, I give unto you power to tread on serpents and scorpions, and over all the power of the enemy: and nothing shall by any means hurt you.

20. Notwithstanding in this rejoice not, that the spirits are subject unto you; but rather rejoice, because your names are written in heaven.

- Luke 10:17-20.

9. Do not be enticed

demons are very cunning. Sometimes they may flatter the deliverance minister or try to send him or her on a guilt trip by mentioning some of the deliverance minister's weaknesses. Sometimes they may sow seeds of discord with intent to have the church or a deliverance team divided. We should always remember they are liars.[11] They are not our legitimate source of information or divine revelation. We only take orders from heaven[12] not hell. Paul and Silas could not take this.

---

[11] John 8:44; 1 Timothy 4:1-2.
[12] Psalm 37:23; Romans 8:14.

16.   And it came to pass, as we went to prayer, a certain damsel possessed with a spirit of divination met us, which brought her masters much gain by soothsaying:

17.   The same followed Paul and us, and cried, saying, These men are the servants of the most high God, which shew unto us the way of salvation.

18.   And this did she many days. But Paul, being grieved, turned and said to the spirit, I command thee in the name of Jesus Christ to come out of her. And he came out the same hour.

- Acts 16:16-18.

10. Do not depend on the arm of flesh

You cannot and should never attempt to use the arm of the flesh to cast demons out.

Slapping or kicking the one you minister deliverance to or spitting upon them is not the scriptural way to cast demons out. That person is as dear to God as you are. Please do not degrade God's people. Our Lord Jesus died in shame so they may be esteemed.

3.   For though we walk in the flesh, we do not war after the flesh:

4.   (For the weapons of our warfare *are* not carnal, but mighty through God to the pulling down of strong holds;)

- 2 Corinthians 10:3-4.

11. Repentance and forgiveness

At times those who need deliverance have been hurt. They may need to be helped and encouraged to forgive those who grieved them.[13]   Repentance and forgiveness pave the way for God to heal our emotional wounds.   Wherever true repentance and forgiveness lacks, the presence of God and the joy of answered prayer is likely to be absent too.

> 25.   And when ye stand praying, forgive, if ye have ought against any: that your Father also which is in heaven may forgive you your trespasses.
>
> 26.   But if ye do not forgive, neither will your Father which is in heaven forgive your trespasses.
>
> - Mark 11:25-26.

> 14.   We know that we have passed from death unto life, because we love the brethren. He that loveth not *his* brother abideth in death.

---

[13] Mathew 5:23–24; Luke 17:3-4.

15. Whosoever hateth his brother is a murderer: and ye know that no murderer hath eternal life abiding in him.

- 1 John 3:14–15.

17. For the kingdom of God is not meat and drink; but righteousness, and peace, and joy in the Holy Ghost.

- Romans 14:17.

12. Wisdom and confidentiality

In many cases those who need deliverance long for someone to confide in. This makes them quite vulnerable.

The deliverance minister should avoid publicizing the secrets told him or her during a session of prayer, counselling, or deliverance. It is also wrong and unpleasant in the sight of God for deliverance minister to take advantage of the person or group of people they minister to by commercializing the gospel or by abusing them sexually. Manipulation is not of God. It belongs to the kingdom of darkness.

It is true that the means by which the gospel is spread are not free but it is also true that our salvation, deliverance and healing have already been paid for by Jesus Christ by the Son of the Living God[14]

One must be very careful when ministering to members of the opposite sex especially if their spouses have wounded them. There is wisdom in always asking a third person to be part of that prayer, counselling, or deliverance session.

The deliverance ministry is a direct confrontation against satan. There is need for you to protect your testimony. No wonder our Lord Jesus always ministered to people in the

---

[14] Isaiah 53:1–12; Matthew 8:16–17; 1 Peter 2:24.

presence of other people. Even where the public was not acceptable, He always went with His trusted team. That way, no would successfully compose a mudslinging story against Him.

35. While he yet spake, there came from the ruler of the synagogue's *house certain* which said, Thy daughter is dead: why troublest thou the Master any further?

36. As soon as Jesus heard the word that was spoken, He saith unto the ruler of the synagogue, Be not afraid, only believe.

37. And He suffered no man to follow Him, save Peter, and James, and John the brother of James.

38.   A cometh to the house of the ruler of the synagogue, and seeth the tumult, and them that wept and wailed greatly.

39.   And when He was come in, He saith unto them, Why make ye this ado, and weep? the damsel is not dead, but sleepeth.

40.   And they laughed Him to scorn. But when He had put them all out, He taketh the father and the mother of the damsel, and them that were with Him, and entereth in where the damsel was lying.

41.   And He took the damsel by the hand, and said unto her, Talitha cumi; which is, being interpreted, Damsel, I say unto thee, arise.

42.   And straightway the damsel arose, and walked; for she was *of the age* of twelve years. And they were astonished with a great astonishment.

43.   And He charged them straitly that no man should know it; and commanded that something should be given her to eat.

- Mark 5:35-43.

That was quite remarkable. Even when He did not want the miracle publicized, He still went with someone for ministry. He stayed away from secret prayer, secret counselling, and secret deliverance rooms. Did He have a home? Yes He did.[15]

---

[15] John 1:35-39.

Chapter 11.

Salvation, deliverance, and healing

Beloved, it is very hard for you to think about overcoming the enemy while you still serve his interests. Just as we have already discussed, repentance is the first step to our liberty because we serve a holy God Who can only be approached according to His terms!

All of us have sinned and come short of the glory of God.[1] No sin is little because the God sinned against is not little. God's Word says;

---

[1] Romans 3:23.

"The soul that sins, it shall die".[2] Left on our own, we all stand condemned, worthy of hell fire.[3]

God in his mercy sent His Son Jesus to show us the way, and to suffer the penalty of our transgressions. It was because of our sins that He was "stricken, smitten of God, and afflicted".[4] He tasted death for everyone.[5] He died for our sins. Every claim of justice against humanity was settled by the Son of God. He was delivered on account of our transgressions and was raised up from the dead when we stood justified, according to the justice of God.

Every sinner who comes to God through Christ is forgiven because their sins were laid upon Him. Being judged in Christ they cannot be found guilty. God the Supreme Judge therefore declares: "There is therefore now no

---

[2] Ezekiel 18:4, 20.
[3] Psalm 9:17; Revelation 21:8.
[4] Isaiah 53:4.
[5] Hebrews 2:9.

condemnation to them which are in Christ Jesus, who walk not after the flesh, but after the Spirit" - Romans 8:1.

> 16. For God so loved the world, that he gave his only begotten Son, that whosoever believeth in him should not perish, but have everlasting life.
>
> - John 3:16.

Jesus, the Son of God was crucified (John 19:14-18). The Son of God did not only die for our sins, He also rose up from the dead,[6] and He lives for ever more.[7] He is the Author of eternal salvation.[8] Our salvation is based upon our faith in Jesus Christ, and in what He did for us by His death and resurrection.[9]

---

[6] 1 Corinthians 15:3-4.
[7] Revelation 1:18.
[8] Hebrews 5:9.
[9] Romans 10:9-11.

He is called the Lamb of God because he bore our sins.[10] He is called our High Priest because *"He ever liveth to make intercession for"* us.[11]

The blood of Christ was shed at Calvary for our redemption.[12] There is sufficient power in the blood of Jesus to deliver us from the kingdom of darkness and to translate us into the Kingdom of His marvellous light.[13] Our salvation includes deliverance, healing, and restoration.[14]

Beloved in Christ, we will all live forever. There are only two eternal places where we will live after our time here on earth. Either with Jesus in the presence of God[15] or with the devil in the lake of fire![16] Where do you plan to spend your eternity?

---

[10] Isaiah 53:4-6; John 1:29; 1 Peter 2:24; 3:18.
[11] Hebrews 7:25.
[12] Ephesians 1:7; Colossians 1:14.
[13] Colossians 1:13; 1 Peter 2:9.
[14] Isaiah 53:4-6.
[15] 1 Thessalonians 4:13-17; Revelation 21:1-7.
[16] Matthew 26:41-46; Revelation 20:11-15; 21:8.

You can make a quality decision to be a friend of God through Christ! By that decision you will have eternal life.[17] You will pass from death to life.[18]

You will be translated from the kingdom of darkness into His marvellous light.[19] Please say the following prayer out loudly and clearly from the bottom of your heart.

"Dear Lord God,

"I acknowledge that I am a sinner, unworthy of your fellowship and promises.

"I know that Your Son, Jesus Christ died for my sins and was raised from the dead for my justification. I know that He is in heaven, seated on Your right hand.

---

[17] John 1:12.
[18] 1 John 3:14-15.
[19] 1 Peter 2:9.

235

"Have mercy upon me. Please forgive me.

"I do now receive and confess Your Son Jesus Christ as my Lord and Saviour.

"Father, thank You so much for my salvation. In the Name of Jesus Christ. Amen".

If you have committed your life to Christ, it will be important for you to belong to a Bible believing Church whose leaders are subject to the written Word of God. They will baptize you by immersion. They will teach the Word of God to you. They will pray for you to be filled with the Holy Spirit. Now you are a believer!

The inward evidence to the believer of their salvation is the direct witness of the Spirit.[20] The outward evidence to all people is a life of righteousness and true holiness. This kind of

---

[20] Romans 8:16.

life rejects such behaviour as homosexuality, lesbianism, sexual immorality and all other sexual perversions, lust, incest, idolatry, envy, murder, strife, drunkenness, deceit, malice, gossip, slander, insolence, arrogance, boasting, promoting evil deeds, disobedience, greed, covetousness, and all forms of moral depravity.[21]

You will need to bear fruit.

> 22. But the fruit of the Spirit is love, joy, peace, longsuffering, gentleness, goodness, faith,

> 23. Meekness, temperance: against such there is no law.
>
> - Galatians 5:22-23.

I pray that you will have a wonderful time living a life of obedience to God. In case we

---

[21] Romans 1:18-32; Colossians 3:5.

do not meet here on earth, we will meet along the golden streets and will for ever rejoice in the presence of our Father. God bless you.

Now you have the right to be free. Please say the following prayer out loudly and clearly meaning it from the very bottom of your heart. There might be wisdom in praying this prayer in the company of someone capable of helping you just in case a need for deliverance may arise.

Dear heavenly Father, I come to you in the Name of Your Son Jesus Christ!

I know that you love me and that you demonstrated Your love by sending Your Son Jesus to pay the supreme price for my redemption.

I acknowledge that I am guilty of the sins in my life and in my ancestors' lives which resulted in curses. I repent of all those sins in the Name of Jesus Christ.

Father, Your Word says I will not be forgiven if I do not forgive those who have wronged me. Father, please give me the grace to forgive in Jesus' Name. I do now forgive all those people who wronged me causing me sorrow. I forgive you … (mention their names and what they did if you can remember it). I declare myself free from the spirit of un-forgiveness in Jesus' Name!

Father, please forgive me for every sin I have committed due to the lust of the flesh, the lust of the eyes and the pride of life. Please forgive me for every evil and careless word which I have spoken or meditated upon. Let the words of my mouth and the meditation of my heart be acceptable in Your sight, O Lord my Strength and my Redeemer in Jesus' Name!

In the Name of Jesus Christ, the Son of the Living God, I repent of all sexual perversions including pornography, sexual fantasies, fornication, adultery, homosexuality, lesbianism, masturbation and all forms of moral depravity whether committed by me or any one of my relatives and covenant friends living or dead.

I repent of all acts of rebellion, disobedience, financial sins, sorcery, divination and all sorts of witchcraft and occult involvement. Please forgive me for every idle word which I have spoken or believed in and every oath or pledge for which I am held responsible. Let me be cleansed by the blood of Your Son Jesus Christ.

Father, Your Word declares that when I confess all my sins, You are faithful and just to forgive me my sins and to cleanse me from all unrighteousness. Basing on Your Word, I acknowledge Your faithfulness and thank You for forgiving me. I stand forgiven. All my sins are remitted in Jesus' Name!

satan, hear this in Jesus Name. I do not belong to you any longer. I am a child of God, saved by His grace and cleansed from all unrighteousness by the blood of Jesus. You have no legal claim over my life any longer.

In the Name of Jesus, I thank You Father for the whole armour which You have provided for me according to the scriptures. Right now I fasten my loins with the belt of truth. I stand having on the breast plate of righteousness. My feet are shod with the preparation of the gospel of peace. Above all I take the shield of faith and right now I declare all the fiery darts of the wicked quenched. I take the helmet of salvation and the sword of the Spirit which is the Word of God. Help me pray with all prayer and supplication in the Spirit, and watching thereunto with all perseverance for all saints. I put on Christ as my garment and let no provision be made whatsoever for the flesh to reign over me. I declare all this in the Name of Jesus Christ.

Father, in the Name of Your Son Jesus Christ, I counter all the petitions of satan and his cohorts against me. The blood of Jesus testifies that I am Your righteousness in Christ, and that I am the apple of Your eye. I thank You Father because You disappoint the devices of the crafty so that their hands cannot perform their enterprises against me. Please do not grant the powers of darkness anything they ask of you concerning me. Let all satan's desires concerning my life, family, friends and property be frustrated in Jesus' Name!

In the Name of Jesus Christ, the Son of the Living God, I break every communication which the astrologers, witches, warlocks, and all wicked beings have with celestial creatures against me. Let every satanic enchantment against me be confounded in Jesus' Name!

In Jesus' Name, I declare the blood of Jesus Christ against every evil sacrifice offered to the powers of darkness against me. Let every satanic altar and all high places raised against me be permanently destroyed in Jesus' Name. Let every demonic device against me be destroyed in Jesus Name.

In the Name of Jesus, I cancel every accusation brought up against me! I cancel every judgment against me by the kingdom of darkness and I nullify every verdict against me by the kingdom of darkness, in the Name of Jesus Christ. I command all panels and committees set up against me to be scattered into oblivion in Jesus' Name! Let every evil voice and tongue against me be permanently silenced by the power of God in Jesus' Name!

In the Name of Jesus Christ the Son of the Living God, I speak to you earth and all earthly beings to reject the voices of witches, warlocks and all wicked beings against me right now. In Jesus' Name I command you water bodies and everything that is in you to reject the voices of witches, warlocks and all wicked beings against me. In the Name of Jesus Christ, the Son of the Living God, I command every spiritual storm and turbulence against me to cease right now.

In the Name of Jesus, I take authority over every work of unrighteousness. In the

Name of Jesus, I renounce every ungodly vow and pledge which I have ever made to satan, to any of his priests, or to anyone living or dead. In Jesus' Name I place under the blood of Jesus, every ungodly pact, agreement, or covenant of which I am part, knowingly or unknowingly, whether it was done by me or anyone living or dead. All those ungodly agreements of which I am part knowingly or unknowingly, whether entered into by the blood of humans, animals, birds, the sap of trees, or any other thing are hereby placed under the blood of Jesus Christ and I declare them permanently broken in the Name of Jesus Christ, the Son of the Living God.

In the Name of Jesus, I take authority over and I break every curse working in my life, or in the lives of any of my family members. I break all curses of failure, poverty, lack, indebtedness, endless financial frustrations, sicknesses and diseases, witchcraft, premature death, vagabond, rejection, abuse, rape, frigidity and family destruction. In the Name of Jesus Christ, I break all curses working against my marriage and children. Let every garment and programme of death imposed upon me be destroyed in Jesus' Name!

In the Name of Jesus Christ, I break myself loose from every curse affecting my life in any way known or unknown to me. I break every hex, jinx, spell, and every negative words spoken over my life and over the lives of all those near and dear to me!

In the Name of Jesus, I defy all the barriers set for me by satan and every ungodly being living or dead. I break every spirit of caging, every fetter, chain, shackle, cord, habit, and evil cycle over my life in Jesus' Name.

I thank You Father that I was redeemed from the curse of the law when my Lord and Saviour Jesus Christ was hanged on the cross at Calvary. Thank You for the blood of Jesus by which my sins are remitted and by which all curses affecting my life have lost their ground.

I thank You Father that I am the temple of God and that the Holy Spirit resides in me. I rejoice in Your truth that I am the apple of Your eye. The power and influence of the devourer is broken over my life. Abraham's blessings are mine. No weapon that is formed against me shall prosper and every evil tongue that rises up against me in judgment shall be permanently defeated in Jesus' Name. I am more than a conqueror through You Who loved me. I am the head and not the tail. I shall not die but live to declare the works of the Lord in Jesus' Name!

Father, in Jesus' Name I thank You because Your divine power has given me all things that pertain unto life and godliness. I have been blessed with all spiritual blessings in heavenly places in Christ. I thank You Father because You supply all my need according to Your riches in glory by Christ Jesus. I bless Your holy Name because You load me with benefits every day.

Father, I agree with you and in the Jesus' Name I declare; my Lord Jesus was wounded for my transgressions, He was bruised for my iniquities, the chastisement of my peace was upon Him and with His stripes I was healed. In Jesus' Name I declare that I have the mind of Christ and I am like a tree that is planted by the streams of water, which yields its fruits in season and whose leaves do not wither. Whatever I do shall prosper because the blessing of God rests upon my life and every work of my hands in Jesus' Name!

In the Name of Jesus Christ the Son of the Living God, I resist you satan. Flee from my life in Jesus Name!

I command all spirits of sexual perversions, self-pity double mindedness, unbelief, caging, evil control of my life, fear, divorce, rejection, ugliness, bondages of all kinds, rage, rape, abuse of every kind, strife, contention, frigidity, impotence, separation, fibroids, cancer, sexual perversions, unnecessary pains during the menstruation periods, widowhood, single-parenthood, spinsterhood, anxiety, despair, sadism, masochism and every evil other spirit mentioned or unmentioned to come out of me in the Name of Jesus Christ!

Let every power passing strange currents into my life be bound in Jesus' Name! Let every attack against me through dreams be frustrated in Jesus' Name! Let every power arrayed against me in the high places, on land, in the waters, in the jungles, or under the earth be bound and broken in Name of Jesus Christ. Let my name be blotted out of every evil register and out of all satanic records in Jesus' Name. Let every doorway used by the enemy against me be closed right now in Jesus' Name. I break every system of communication used by the powers of darkness against me in Jesus' Name!

In the Name of Jesus the Son of the Living God I declare civil strife and great confusion in the camp of every principality, power, rulers of darkness of this world and wicked spirits in high places which operate against me. In the Name of Jesus, I tread upon all serpents, scorpions and every power of the enemy, and I declare that nothing shall by any means hurt me.

I declare today that I am a child of God, purchased by the blood of the Lamb. Lord, I thank You for my salvation, deliverance and healing in the Name of Jesus' Christ!

It is important to note that some demons are stubborn and may require an anointed, experienced deliverance minister to help you even after the prayer you just said. One thing remains true, all their covenants are broken, and every legal claim satan had over your life is null and void. You are free in Jesus' Name. Hallelujah for the blood of Jesus Christ, the Lamb of God!

Chapter 12.

How to maintain your deliverance

I have almost copied this chapter verbatim from the seventh chapter of my book; *"Spiritual Female Problems"* because the truths contained therein serve the same purpose as in this case.

It is very painful for a person to be touched by the power of God only to return to their bondage a few moments later. The truth that a demon has been cast out of a person is no guarantee that satan has lost interest in that person. The Lord Jesus taught us that evil spirits are desperate for flesh and blood. They will try to do anything within their limited ability to repossess any house they may have been thrown out of!

43. When the unclean spirit is gone out of a man, he walketh through dry places, seeking rest, and findeth none.

44. Then he saith, i will return into my house from whence i came out; and when he is come, he findeth *it* empty, swept, and garnished.

45. Then goeth he, and taketh with himself seven other spirits more wicked than himself, and they enter in and dwell there: and the last *state* of that man is worse than

the first. Even so shall it be also unto this wicked generation.

- Matthew 12:43-45.

There is need for you to establish a firewall so no power of darkness can ever have access to your life again. I have discovered some twelve keys in God's Word that will help you keep your deliverance.

1.   Salvation

The first and most important key to enjoying any blessing from God is Salvation. You cannot have access to God's covenant blessings until you surrender to Jesus to be your Lord and Saviour! There cannot be any other better foundation for your life and plans except Christ.[1]

Anyone good or evil can obtain a miracle from

---

[1] 1 Corinthians 3:11.

God.[2] However, the power to keep a miracle is a reserve of only those who are in a covenant relationship with God; His children saved by the grace.

The promises of God are conditional. They always bear an "IF".[3] We need to be born into the family of God so we may have the right to His promises.

The Kingdom of God is righteousness, peace, and joy in the Holy Ghost.[4] Except a person be born again, he or she cannot see the Kingdom of God.[5]

2.　God's Word

It is very important to have a Bible of your own and to study it regularly. The enemy of your

---

[2] Matthew 5:44-45.
[3] 2 Chronicles 7:14.
[4] Romans 14:17.
[5] John 3:3.

soul; satan is not scared of your words, talents and skills. he is defeated by the Word of the Living God. We are encouraged to soak ourselves into God's Word and let it be part of our lives.[6]

> 8.   This book of the law shall not depart out of thy mouth; but thou shalt meditate therein day and night, that thou mayest observe to do according to all that is written therein: for then thou shalt make thy way prosperous, and then thou shalt have good success..
>
> -   Joshua 1:8.

Good success has its roots in the Word of God. That is one of the reasons we should spend time studying God's Word.

> 16.   Let the word of Christ dwell in you richly in all wisdom; teaching

---

[6] John 15:7

255

and admonishing one another in psalms and hymns and spiritual songs, singing with grace in your hearts to the Lord.

- Colossians 3:16.

The Word of God is our bread.[7] We need to feed on this heavenly bread so we may grow and be victorious.

3.   Church

It is important to find a Bible believing, Bible practising congregation and be part of it. They will baptize you by immersion into water and pray for you to be filled with the Holy Spirit. They will teach the principles of God to you as revealed in His Word.

God's Word encourages us not to be churchless. It is the privilege and obligation of

---

[7] Deuteronomy 8:3, John 6:31-35.

every child of God to belong to a God glorifying church. There are quite a number of things you will only overcome when you join yourself to people who love and obey God.

God has established divine leadership in the church.[8] You will grow and be victorious with their Bible based counsel and spiritual covering.

> 25.   Not forsaking the assembling of ourselves together, as the manner of some *is*; but exhorting *one another.* and so much the more, as ye see the day approaching.
>
>   - Hebrews 10:25.

4.   Prayer

Prayer builds your fellowship with God. It is easier for a prayerful Christian to exercise the

---

[8] Ephesians 4:11-14.

power of God than a prayerless one. God empowers those who wait upon Him in prayer.[9] There are challenges and temptations which never come your way just because you prayed.[10] We are encouraged to pray without ceasing.

17.   Pray without ceasing.

- 1 Thessalonians 5:17.

We should pray with all prayer and supplication in the Spirit.[11] Whenever we pray we breath the presence of God into our lives. His presence hovers upon those who wait upon Him in prayer.

Once we are filled with the Holy Ghost and we continue praying in tongues we build ourselves up on our most holy faith.[12] We should pray with our understanding and in

---

[9] Isaiah 40:29-31.
[10] Matthew 26:41; Mark 14:38.
[11] Ephesians 6:18.
[12] Jude 20.

tongues.

> 14.   For if I pray in an *unknown* tongue, my spirit prayeth, but my understanding is unfruitful.

> -   1 Corinthians 14:14.

Prayerlessness is a kind of pride against the Person of God. A prayerless person lives their life as though they have all the wisdom and power to deal with life's issues and so do not need God's grace. Prayerless people are an easy prey for the devil.

Prayerlessness also makes a person beastlike and causes the wrath of God to come upon that person's life.[13]

5.   The Blood of Jesus

There is awesome power in the blood of

---

[13] Jeremiah 10:20-25.

Jesus. In the Old Testament Job used to keep his family safe from every attack of satan by shedding the blood of animals. A hedge of protection was established around his family which satan could not easily break through was it not for Job's fears.

On one occasion God challenged satan about Job's life and satan outlined five things which discouraged him as far as Job's life was concerned. In Job 1:10 there is a point after every punctuation mark.

> 10. Hast not thou made an hedge about him, and about his house, and about all that he hath on every side? thou hast blessed the work of his hands, and his substance is increased in the land.
>
> - Job 1:10.

Whenever Job shed the blood of animals:

a. A hedge of protection was established around him.

b. A hedge of protection was established around his household (family).

c. A hedge of protection was established around his investments and resources on every side.

d. There was a blessing which came upon the work of his hands.

e. His substance would be increased in the land.

If the blood of animals did so much for an Old Testament servant of God, how much more shall the blood of Christ do for God's children? Every time we declare the blood of Jesus Christ, the attacks of satan are thwarted (I encourage you to get my book; *"The Blood that speaketh better things"*).

6. Close every satanic inlet

It is very important for you to identify the areas where your need for deliverance was and every doorway which the powers of darkness used to enter into your life. Make a quality decision to close them permanently. For example, if someone lonely used to be a prostitute it may not be the best decision for that person to be the sole counsellor of a lonely lecher in a dark solitary place.

satan is crafty and quite persistent. Once you allow him a place in your life, he will take advantage of it to your destruction. Close every doorway and do not allow him to recapture any of those areas in your life where he has been defeated.

43. When the unclean spirit is gone out of a man, he walketh through dry places, seeking rest, and findeth none.

44.   Then he saith, I will return into my house from whence I came out; and when he is come, he findeth *it* empty,   swept,   and garnished.

45.   Then goeth he, and taketh with himself seven other spirits more wicked than himself, and they enter in and dwell there: and the last *state* of that man is worse than the first. Even so shall it be also unto this wicked generation.

- Matthew 12:43-45.

Go and sin no more lest that which is worse comes upon you![14]

7.   Apply the mind of Christ

---

[14] John 5:14.

As a child of God, your mind should be renewed by the Word of God on a regular basis so that you may not be enslaved to any unholy thoughts bred in hell.[15]

> 8. Finally, brethren, whatsoever things are true, whatsoever things *are* honest, whatsoever things *are* just, whatsoever things *are* pure, whatsoever things *are* lovely, whatsoever things *are* of good report; if *there be* any virtue, and if *there be* any praise, think on these things.
>
> - Philippians 4:8.

One of the quickest means of becoming an enemy of God is to have a carnal mind.[16]

---

[15] Romans 12:2; James 1:21.
[16] Romans 8:6-8.

We have the mind of Christ.[17] God has given us the Spirit of power, love and a sensible, sober, sound mind.[18] We should exercise it all the time. Let the words of our mouths and the meditations of our hearts be acceptable to God.[19] The words of our mouths affect the meditations of our hearts *(subconscious mind)*. Every child of God, therefore has a need and to always speak words that will program their subconscious mind for victorious living.

When your mind is renewed, you become a candidate of God's blessings and true prosperity.[20] There is need to bring into captivity every thought to the obedience of Christ.[21]

8. Remain sober and vigilant

There will be need for you to be sober and

---

[17] 1 Corinthians 2:16
[18] 2 Timothy 1:7
[19] Psalms 19:14.
[20] Psalms 1:1-3; 3 John 2
[21] 2 Corinthians 10:5.

vigilant all the time.[22] This becomes very easy if you dress up in the whole armour of God all the time.[23] The armour of God builds a very strong firewall around you so that no demon can touch you.

God has given us authority to deny satan a place in our lives. So, neither give place to the devil.[24]

> 8. Be sober, be vigilant; because your adversary the devil, as a roaring lion, walketh about, seeking whom he may devour:
>
> - 1 Peter 5:8.

9. Rebuke satan as a person

The Lord Jesus rebuked satan and demons on a number of occasions.[25] satan is not an idea. satan is a person. he is an eternally

---

[22] 1 Peter 5:8.
[23] Ephesians 6:10-18
[24] Ephesians 4:27.
[25] Matthew 16:23; 17:18.

defeated foe.[26] In the midst of His temptations the Lord Jesus spoke God's Word to satan and satan's schemes failed.[27] That is what a child of God should do.

Whenever any temptation comes your way trying to drag you into your sinful past, remember it is satan's snare so he can have access to your life once again. Learn to say out loudly and clearly: *"satan, I resist you in the Name of Jesus Christ".* When you resist the devil, he will flee from you.[28]

> 9.   Whom resist stedfast in the faith, knowing that the same afflictions are accomplished in your brethren that are in the world.
>
> -   1 Peter 5:9.

Do not allow those old habits to take advantage of you again. Do not allow sin to

---

[26] 1 Corinthians 2:6-8; Colossians 2:15; Hebrews 2:14.
[27] Matthew 4:3-11.
[28] James 4:7.

be your Lord any longer.[29]

10. Agree with people of like faith in prayer

18. Verily I say unto you, Whatsoever ye shall bind on earth shall be bound in heaven: and whatsoever ye shall loose on earth shall be loosed in heaven.

19. Again I say unto you, That if two of you shall agree on earth as touching any thing that they shall ask, it shall be done for them of my Father which is in heaven.

20. For where two or three are gathered together in my name, there am I in the midst of them.

- Matthew 18:18-20.

---

[29] Romans 6:14.

You can always bind the demons on assignment against you, on a daily basis. You have authority to loose the angels of God to minister to you[30] and to defeat every evil spirit against you.

The Lord Jesus said He could have asked the Father for twelve legions of angels when attacked.[31] By that time, Judas Ischariot had left them. Him and the remaining eleven disciples made a team of twelve people. So there would be a legion for each of them. Indeed God is no respecter of persons.[32] Whatever He could do for Jesus, He desires to do for us because He loves us just like He loves Christ.[33]

11. Take your place in Christ and reign with Him

---

[30] Hebrews 1:14.
[31] Matthew 26:53.
[32] Acts 10:34.
[33] John 17:22-23.

Ignorance limits a person so they cannot fully enjoy what is rightfully theirs. There is need for you to know who you are in Christ and what fully belongs to you because of the finished work of Christ at Calvary.

Remember to learn those verses in the New Testament, especially in the epistles which reveal to you who you are in Christ and what belongs to you as a result of Calvary. Those verses which bear phrases such as the following; *"in Whom"*, *"through Him"*, *"in Christ"*, *"in Him"*. There is great wisdom in learning them by heart and declaring them in season and out of season.[34]

Whatever a believer declares is established.[35] You can change your environment and reign over sin, devils, and diseases by the words

---

[34] 2 Timothy 4:2.
[35] Job 22:28; Mark 11:23.

you speak.[36]

12. Do the work of an evangelist

One does not have to be an evangelist in order to preach the gospel. We have all been called to do the work of an evangelist. That is one of the easiest ways for you to make full proof of whatever calling and ministry God has entrusted you with.[37]

When a person proclaims the gospel, they are exercising their God given authority over satan. It is part of our spiritual warfare as children of God.[38]

Proclaiming the good news means you will have to testify about Christ. Whenever you testify about Christ here on earth, He too testifies about you before the Father and before the holy angels of God.[39]

---

[36] Proverbs 18:21.
[37] 2 Timothy 4:5.
[38] Ephesians 6:15.
[39] Matthew 10:32-33; Luke 12:8-9.

When you testify about the resurrection of Christ, great grace comes upon you.[40]

There are blessings which come upon your life just because you have proclaimed the gospel.[41] So arise snd proclaim the good news of our risen Lod and Saviour Jesus Christ; the Son of the Living God.

═══════════════════════

Beloved in Christ, in case this book has been a blessing to you, please write a good review about it on www.amazon.com so that others may be encouraged to read it as well.

Your brother in Christ,

Moses Nsubuga Sekatawa.

---

[40] Acts 4:33.
[41] Isaiah 52:7.

Other books by Moses Nsubuga Sekatawa:

1. Spiritual female problems.
2. Have some money.
3. Now faith is
4. Worshipping God with our resources.
5. The Blood that speaketh better things.
6. Demolishing evil foundations.

Moses Nsubuga Sekatawa's books are available on www.amazon.com

Made in the USA
Middletown, DE
30 July 2020